Bourdieu, Language and the Media

Bourdieu, Language and the Media

John F. Myles
School of Humanities and Social Sciences
University of East London

First published 2010 by
PALGRAVE MACMILLAN

Palgrave Macmillan in the UK is an imprint of Macmillan Publishers Limited,
registered in England, company number 785998, of Houndmills, Basingstoke,
Hampshire RG21 6XS.

Palgrave Macmillan in the US is a division of St Martin's Press LLC,
175 Fifth Avenue, New York, NY 10010.

Palgrave Macmillan is the global academic imprint of the above companies
and has companies and representatives throughout the world.

Palgrave® and Macmillan® are registered trademarks in the United States,
the United Kingdom, Europe and other countries.

ISBN 978–0–230–22209–0   hardback

This book is printed on paper suitable for recycling and made from fully
managed and sustained forest sources. Logging, pulping and manufacturing
processes are expected to conform to the environmental regulations of the
country of origin.

A catalogue record for this book is available from the British Library.

A catalog record for this book is available from the Library of Congress.

10   9   8   7   6   5   4   3   2   1
19   18   17   16   15   14   13   12   11   10

Printed and bound in Great Britain by
CPI Antony Rowe, Chippenham and Eastbourne

To my parents – Marie and Walter

Contents

List of Figures

List of Tables and Boxes

Acknowledgements

Thanks to: Sue my wife for her support and encouragement and my children Alice and Klinten. *The Manchester Evening News* for permission to reproduce the reports and photographs appearing in Chapters 4 and 5. YouGov for permission to reproduce the poll tables and questions appearing in Chapter 7. The editors and reviewers of *The Sociological Review* for their comments on an earlier version of Chapter 7 which appeared as 'Making Don't Knows Make Sense' (Vol. 56.1, pp. 102–16). The editors and reviewers of the *Journal of Communication Inquiry* for their comments on an earlier version of Chapter 6 which appeared as 'Carnival Radio: Soca-Calypso Music and Afro-Caribbean Voice' (Vol. 24.1, pp. 87–112). Maggie Humm and Derek Robbins at the University of East London. Christabel Scaife, Catherine Mitchell and Jo North at Palgrave Macmillan. Nick Couldry at Goldsmiths College, Bridget Fowler at the University of Glasgow. And Michael Dillon and Scott Lash for great support during my time as a postgraduate student and researcher at Lancaster University.

Introduction

This book has three main aims. Firstly, it argues that media and communication studies has largely neglected Bourdieu's approach to language and power presented in the essays contained in the book *Language and Symbolic Power* (Bourdieu and Thompson 1991). Essentially, that book has been seen as an intervention into theoretical debates in linguistics and neglected by media studies which has preferred to relate Bourdieu's later ideas (Bourdieu 1998) to the field. The present study argues that Bourdieu's concern with giving a sociological account of language actually has great relevance for understanding language in the media. In fact, most discussions of Bourdieu's work in media studies have been conducted at a highly abstract theoretical and conceptual level. For example, Chapter 2 argues that the key recent book on this topic by Benson and Neveu (2005) hardly touches on language, preferring to follow Bourdieu's idea of the 'field' of journalism as a 'topography' of positions. There have also been no book-length studies of how Bourdieu's ideas on language relate to key topics in language and media research. This book aims to fill this gap in the literature, and to offer a timely overview and application of Bourdieu's understanding of language and symbolic power in relation to key contemporary trends in the mass media and communication technologies, as well as seeing how it stands up to major competing perspectives on this topic such as ethnomethodology (Hutchby 2006) and critical discourse analysis (CDA) (Chouliaraki and Fairclough 1999a).

Secondly, this book engages with topics that are recognized as being key traditional areas of concern in the study of language and the media, for example, radio, photography and journalism. However, the book aims to make Bourdieu's original ideas on topics such as photography and journalism, generated at a much earlier period, relevant for students of twenty-first-century media and communication. Alongside this concern, however, this book also relates Bourdieu's approach to relatively new areas of study, such as mobile technologies and media and internet polling.

Thirdly, this book engages with the problem of developing Bourdieu's sociology to take more account of lay knowledgeability or reflexivity. Bourdieu has been heavily criticized for his failure to articulate more 'subjectivist' principles into his work, but this study argues at a number of points that there are resources in his work which can be articulated to meet this problem.

Part I of this book is made up of Chapters 1–3 and is concerned with outlining the key theoretical concerns associated with Bourdieu's approach to language and the media. Chapter 1 reviews Bourdieu's key writings on the topic of language and symbolic power. Essentially, Bourdieu applies a sociological approach to understanding language as an aspect of broader social struggles, and the media therefore plays a subordinate, but relatively autonomous, role in these struggles. This chapter gives an overview of Bourdieu's key ideas on language (*Language and Symbolic Power*) and the social uses of technology (*Photography: a Middle-brow Art*), and his later work on the media (*On Television*). Key ideas ('symbolic power', 'linguistic domination', 'habitus', 'doxa', 'field') are related to issues in language and the media. The chapter moves on to argue that, whilst Bourdieu offers very little direct advice about how language and the media might be studied, his ideas can be usefully applied in this field of study.

Chapter 2 looks at Benson and Neveu's study of the journalistic field (Benson and Neveu 2005) and also other key works which have a bearing on the media from a Bourdieusian perspective such as Wacquant's study of the public sphere (Wacquant and Bourdieu 2005). This chapter also examines Champagne's work on opinion polling (Champagne 1990, 1999), and Crossley's edited collection (Habermas et al. 2004). These key works on Bourdieu, however, all essentially neglect the focus on language which is maintained in this book.

Chapter 3 seeks to address some of the key criticisms of Bourdieu's approach to language that have come from critical discourse studies (Fairclough 2001), and postmodernists like Butler (Butler 1997) and gender and language studies (Adkins and Skeggs 2004). In demonstrating for readers the importance of Bourdieu's approach as a real alternative to critical discourse analysis, sociolinguistics, and ethnomethodology, and elsewhere – Habermas's discourse ethics (in chapter 4), symbolic interactionism and Barthes's semiotics (chapter 5) – the book addresses theoretical issues which will be of concern to readers interested in language and discourse study of the media.

Chapter 3 also develops Bourdieu's approach in order to account for how subordinate or lay discourses groups challenge 'symbolic violence' in the media. For example, as Chapter 8 argues, text messaging can be seen as an important medium of linguistic struggle. This 'lay' or 'mundane' focus of Bourdieu, found in his later work (Bourdieu 1999) is fleshed out in relation to the more phenomenological aspects of Bourdieu's theory and in an encounter with ethnomethodology and Bakhtinian ideas. There are similar theoretical encounters in this book, such as in Chapter 6 where Barthes's idea of 'grain of voice' appears, which are assessed and related to Bourdieu's own concepts such as habitus and 'language market'.

The case study chapters that follow Chapter 3 in Part II are expositions of how Bourdieu's ideas can be deployed in case studies of traditional mass media or more recent developments in digital media. But in all of these chapters the reader will be able to see how Bourdieu's ideas can help us to engage with contemporary debates about language and the media. Chapter 6 draws on primary research interviews with community and established radio broadcasters in order to illustrate how his distinctive approach can be used to analyse language and the mass media. Additional material drawn from secondary sources, such as newspaper reports and photojournalism, and internet polling surveys are also analysed in these chapters in order to produce a more comprehensive understanding of these topics.

City evening press news reports are used in Chapter 4, which examines urban regeneration reporting in relation to issues in contemporary journalistic discourse. Debates over the role of local press in urban regeneration are an important focus for media research (Franklin and Murphy 1991; Logan and Molotch 1987) and also a vital focus for understanding symbolic power. Drawing on Bourdieu's scattered ideas on journalism in his political 'interventions' (Bourdieu et al. 2008), this chapter examines 'paralogism' in urban and regeneration reporting, as well as broader issues clustering around ideas of 'rights to the city'. Quoting from reports, this chapter argues that public deliberation on planning issues is constrained by the form of the 'regeneration story', which prioritizes the interests of 'urban growth coalitions' whilst marginalizing lay and alternative viewpoints.

Chapter 5 examines photojournalistic images in the local press as another site of symbolic power in the reporting of urban regeneration. Bourdieu's essentially sociological (almost anthropological) approach to photography argues that social norms 'organize the photographic valuation of the world [and] what is and isn't photographable' (Bourdieu 1990c). In this light, local press photojournalism is shown to adopt consistently different framings and treatment of elites and lay individuals or community groups. Bourdieu's ideas on embodiment are related to other work on the photographic 'gaze' (demeanour, typologies of facial expression, e.g. Solomon-Godeau 1991) in order to reveal the social codes, and forces, at work in press photojournalism.

Chapters 4 and 5 should be read together as a case study of the role of the city press in urban regeneration reporting. The two chapters also give an alternative way of 'positioning' the local press in the field of the media, and in its relationship to the state (or local forms of governance) than was understood by Bourdieu himself. In *Distinction* Bourdieu argued that (in France) the local press was essentially a politically 'bland' product because it needs to avoid creating controversy (Bourdieu 1984: 442). Bourdieu's readership focus in this part of his study of the cultural field in France goes on to argue that because the working class were more likely to read the popular press, which has an 'omnibus' character that overwhelms serious reporting with popular or entertaining content, they are less likely to be influenced by the political opinions underlying these papers – in contrast to middle-class readers who read 'informative' papers (Bourdieu 1984: 444). However, evening newspapers in the UK are generally read by all classes because only very few cities, such as Liverpool, have two rival papers. Due to this, the two chapters on this topic focus on how the way in which different classes 'appear' in the evening press can be understood relationally, in photojournalism and the language of the reports themselves.

Drawing on interviews and other research data, Chapter 6 depicts a 'topology' of positions in the field of talk radio (public service broadcasting, community, pirate and commercial stations). This chapter also acts as a critical engagement with ethnomethodological studies of talk radio which have dominated this field (Hutchby 1996). The main Bourdieusian argument, as outlined in Chapter 3, that ethnomethodology lacks an adequate sociological grounding is applied to analyse talk and music radio. Radio programming, particularly talk radio, is therefore analysed as a 'site' of social and cultural classificatory activity. At the same time, Bourdieu's approach is supplemented by complementary ideas, such as Barthes's concept of 'voice' (the role of music and speech in creating an identifiable cultural 'persona' or, in Bourdieu's view, 'position') and cultural 'hybridization' (Bhabha 1994; Gilroy 2000).

In the chapters that follow, attention is turned to more recent developments in the media, particularly digital media. Books on the impact of the internet on communication have been dominated by sociolinguistic approaches (Crystal 2001) whilst political accounts of the net have been dominated by postmodernists (Rheingold 2000). However, Chapter 7 questions the claims for the internet as a new, free and open forum for political communication and popular participation or deliberation in politics – in this case media and internet polling. Since Walter Lippman in the 1920s, the relationship between mass media, PR and the opinion polling industry has been a key focus for media studies. This chapter develops Bourdieu's original ideas (Bourdieu 1993b) on opinion polls in order to see how it might be possible to articulate working-class, or 'lay', opinion more successfully. This chapter engages with this issue by examining a recent popular trend in digital mass media – 'internet polling'. However, although often seen as offering a more appropriate avenue for the expression of popular political opinion, the supposedly universal language of the questions used in internet polls is shown to have continuities with the 'exclusion bias' in polls that Bourdieu originally identified. Thus, although internet polling may be popular, class power and larger structures of linguistic and symbolic power militate against its participatory democratic impulses. The chapter illustrates this by quoting some of the questions used in these polls whilst, also, elaborating ideas of 'identification bids' (Lipari 2000) and 'cultural standing' (Strauss 2004) as alternatives.

In Chapter 8 the theoretical issues addressed in Chapter 3 in relation to postmodernism, ethnomethodology, linguistics and sociolinguistics are revisited in relation to the topic of text messaging. Although Bourdieu says very little about the impact of new technologies on class and cultural relations, his ideas can nevertheless help us to analyse language in new media, such as in the case of the mobile phone and text messaging. The chapter analyses mobile telephony in an engagement with ethnomethodology, sociolinguistics and also in relation to McLuhan and the Toronto School. In regard to the latter, the idea of there being a telegraphic/telephonic 'third wave' (following writing and print) of communications media, which has multiplied the speed and delivery of text (McLuhan 2001), can nevertheless be related to lay practices in language that might be enabled by new technologies. This chapter therefore suggests that mobile telephony and text messaging are good examples of how 'mundane text' (Kress 1997: 294) practices in this field may arise and enable challenges to standard language. This 'electronic textual' challenge to standardization in print and written language can be seen as being enabled by the ephemeral nature (wiping, diffused pixelated, anti-materiality) of electronic text. In contrast to postmodern approaches (Rheingold 2002), this chapter stresses the class dimensions of this trend, its appeal to young working-class people who are happy to exploit the essential 'arbitrariness' of the rules of language.

Finally, in the conclusion to this book the key arguments made in the foregoing chapters are revisited and underlined with particular reference to some of the critical issues of reflexivity and method that arise in relation to applying Bourdieu's ideas to language and the media.

Part I Theoretical Issues in Studying Language and the Media

1
Bourdieu–Language–Media

In applying Bourdieu's ideas on language, power and symbolic violence to a number of case studies of contemporary media, this book ranges across various institutions and genres characterizing broadcast media such as talk radio, print media (including journalism and photojournalism), and digital and electronic media such as mobile telephony and the internet. The concern in the following case studies is to interrogate contemporary media in terms of its role in instituting symbolic violence in its practices, whether they be in traditional or new media. The crucial aim of this book is to use Bourdieu's sociology in the way he preferred towards the end of his life, as a critical intervention or what he calls a:

> Combat sport against various forms of symbolic violence that can be exerted against citizens, in particular, and very often these days, through the field of the media. (Benson and Neveu 2005: 29)

Deploying Bourdieu's sociological approach to language in the field of media in this critical way means engaging with the problem of how the media is implicated in broader linguistic (or more generally *symbolic*), struggles over the nature and 'control' of the language itself.

This book will draw upon Bourdieu's ideas on language from a number of key writings by him. However, Bourdieu's particular studies of the press and media, seen in *On Television and Journalism* and his essay in Benson and Neveu's book *Bourdieu and the Journalistic Field*, are not the key sources for the approach contained in this book. Although ideas in these books are referred to in this and the following

9

chapter, generally the underlying position is adapted from the essays contained in *Language and Symbolic Power*. Bourdieu also makes scattered references to journalism and the media in other key works, such as *Distinction* where local journalism (discussed in Chapter 4 of this book) is examined (Bourdieu 1984: 442). But in *Language and Symbolic Power* Bourdieu contrasts his sociological approach to language to that of structuralism, ethnomethodology and sociolinguistics, and these remain the key perspectives on the topic of language and the media, and ones that a Bourdieusian approach needs to primarily address. So in turning to this source, one that has recently been seen as unreasonably neglected in cultural and media studies (Couldry 2003a), and revisiting it in many ways, this book re-encounters these approaches from Bourdieu's distinctive, critical, position.

One of Bourdieu's main arguments in *Language and Symbolic Power* is that Saussure's (Saussure et al. 1983) concern with the 'synchronic' relations of language as an abstract system ('langue') seriously undermines the social significance of the fundamentally *oral* nature of language. The theoretical repercussions of this are quite wide and are discussed in more detail in Chapter 3, but essentially Bourdieu underlines the social relations that influence language and how it is subject to infinite variability as a result. Language is therefore as much a marker of social *distinction* as semantic sense:

> However great the proportion of the functioning of a language that is not subject to variation, there exists, in the area of pronunciation, diction and even grammar, a whole set of differences associated with social differences which, though negligible in the eyes of the linguist, are pertinent from the sociologist's standpoint because they belong to a system of linguistic oppositions which is the *re-translation* of a system of social differences. (Bourdieu and Thompson 1991: 54)

This contrasts to Saussure's structuralist stipulation that the key to the study of language should be its ahistorical, synchronic relations, the 'rules' of language that are largely uninfluenced by time and place. For Bourdieu this comes at the cost of losing sight of the primary role of language in its 'practical state' as spoken discourse which marks out class, status, gender and other social cleavages as well as variables amongst these such as age.

Wherever spoken language and issues of social inequality arise, either as reported in the media or as aspects of the media as an institution in society, usually the concepts of accent, dialect and voice are central to such debates. In nearly all nation states (except for bilingual states like Canada, but these have their own particular issues) linguistic variations within a mother tongue are chiefly marked by variations in accent and dialect. Variations in spoken language remain one of the most pervasive, almost intuitive, means of social classification in modern societies. As the following quote shows, variations in spoken language thus make us unconsciously 'position' ourselves against others:

> The expectation of inarticulacy, based on someone's appearance or accent, is one of the most powerful prejudices there is (I should know, I'm from Birmingham). People who expect, and are expected, to have no voice of their own collude with the status quo precisely to avoid communicating openly and thereby expose the full extent of their disadvantage. (*The Guardian*, 4 March 2008)

Sociolinguistics identifies this by the term 'diglossia', but in Bourdieu's terms it is the result of the imposition of 'symbolic violence', the power of the dominant class working though cultural forms, upon a subordinated language community. Historically, in the UK Received Pronunciation (RP), in the USA, 'General American' (GA), and 'High German' in Germany are the standards which set the basis for pronunciation or spelling (when lexicographers draw on the standard pronunciation as the basis for phonetic spelling) in written language. It is also no coincidence that the fonts of individual letters in print are commonly referred to as 'characters', indicating the socially arbitrary origins of the phoneticized spelling of most words.

From an anthropological perspective, Hanks has argued that 'linguistic reasoning' is central to Bourdieu's views on society and nearly all of his ideas are actually 'filtered through it' (Hanks 2005: 69). Hanks points out that Bourdieu understands language as being structured between discourse in context and the linguistic field itself:

> Whereas 'discourse context' [...] is the surround of an utterance or form, the field with its boundaries assumes no discursive act at its centre. It exists prior to and apart from any particular utterance or engagement and is in this sense objective. (Hanks 2005: 74)

This suggests that the linguistic field has something of the status of Saussure's 'langue' but Bourdieu sees the 'expressive interest', parole, as the context-dependent variable whilst the 'social capacity' to speak is derived from the socio-structural 'capacities' of the field that effects symbolic violence, not the language 'system' itself. Hanks also makes the point that even at the level of parole or the 'deictic field' (speaker, addressee and frames/topics) there is relative autonomy insofar as it is:

> Defined by language, but non-autonomous in those features such as reference, description, illocutionary force, and indication are recast as ways of taking up positions in the field. (Hanks 2005: 75)

Hanks is also concerned with how Bourdieu's approach might account for the way speakers can reflectively grasp their own engagement in language (Hanks 2005: 69) at this level. He therefore reminds us that there are 'indexical parameters' of language at the level of parole even if the field structures such features of the language as 'stylistic hierarchies' (Hanks 2005: 75). This means one must always think of language as something 'in action', in contexts, even though the concern with symbolic power is to underline how the structures work.

Bourdieu sees the apparent 'permanency' of the rules of spelling, 'correct' pronunciation and grammar as the result of social struggles between different class groups over language (Bourdieu and Thompson 1991: 45). The rules of grammar are thus never politically innocent standards written into dictionaries, in educational standards or in the media, but historically and socially arbitrary. So 'sociologically pertinent linguistic differences' such as those marking the working class in the UK who do not use 'Received Pronunciation', are a much more important focus for Bourdieu than applying the numerous and highly technical terms of the various branches of linguistics (i.e. phonetics). The highly detailed phoneticizing of spoken language found in sociolinguistic texts is absent in this book. However, as Bourdieu states, if this means 'lack of technical sophistication' then 'one must pay a higher price for truth while accepting a lower profit of distinctions' (Bourdieu and Thompson 1991: 34).

Like language, the media is also a field that is constituted by processes of social distinction and strategies of class control. But just where the media field lies in relation to the social field will also be the result of demographic trends influencing the professions associated with it.

Thus a recent study of the opportunities for entering the profession of journalism found that of journalism students:

> Fewer than 10% came from any kind of working-class background, and only 3% from semi-skilled or unskilled occupations. [...] 'walk through our corridors' a lecturer at one university journalism school told me, 'and you will hear that homogeneous public school accent'. (*The Guardian*, 7 April 2008)

We can also see such class aspects of the media in relation to the recent BBC TV drama on working-class culture entitled *White Girl* which ended up merely perpetuating demeaning working-class stereotypes ('chavs') which it had hoped to avoid:

> The trouble with all this wasn't just that it felt so simplistic (chavs bad, Muslims good). It also led to a drama that managed to be both unbelievable and boringly predictable at the same time. And, because the characters remained locked in their preordained emblematic roles, their dilemmas never seemed either real or engaging. (*Daily Telegraph*, 11 March 2008)

In Chapter 5 of this book we will examine photojournalistic images of working-class people. The media's processes of representation of different social groups are highly charged with symbolic power, and when examined in this way reveal underlying deep cultural contradictions. In relation to film, the problem of how a mainly middle-class medium charges itself with representing the working class is criticized here by the novelist Irvine Welsh:

> In Danny Boyle's film of Trainspotting, and now Paul McGuigan's The Acid House, [...] my concerns have been largely with young working class males. It is a highly underwritten culture, and it never fails to amaze me that for a section of society that's derided as unhip, unsavoury and uncultured, the middle-classes and their media seem desperate to appropriate almost everything that comes from it. (*The Guardian*, 16 May 1999)

The way that working-class accents and dialects are articulated in the media to represent them and at the same time works to associate them with particular moral attributes is discussed in some detail in Chapter 4 on urban regeneration reporting.

This sociological tenet of Bourdieu's confrontation with structural linguistics is the key to his approach to understanding language as infused with relations of symbolic power. His focus on the 'socially significant' aspects of spoken language, particularly its 'paralinguistic' or phonetic aspects such as dialect, accent and voice, has been under-utilized in the analysis of language and the media (see Chapter 2). Bourdieu is concerned with how social differences in spoken language, 'isoglosses' of accent and dialect and grammar, influence meaning and correspond to differences in status and power. Thus the whole gamut of features often related to the embodied dimensions of talk such as 'voice', prosody, intonation, 'hesitancy' and other paralinguistic features such as hand movements and lexical differences in vocabulary, are important for analysing the media using this approach.

As noted above, Bourdieu is more concerned with the connotative aspects of language, as 'parole', and rejects the 'internalist' forms of analysis associated with sociolinguistics. Sociolinguistics' large technical glossary can help it identify quite minute phonetic variations in spoken discourse. But Bourdieu argues that sociolinguists over-technicize phonetic variations 'noting differences where ordinary speakers hear none' (Bourdieu and Thompson 1991: 89). Instead, Bourdieu argues that a mother tongue's standard form is the key stake over which different social forces compete. Bourdieu argues that we need to see how such language wars arise as a function of our fundamentally social impulse to compete for status, not just 'in' language but more broadly in terms of 'symbolic power'. Thus, the particular differences in working-class accents in, say, Liverpool or Norwich in the UK identified by sociolinguistics are less important for Bourdieu than what unifies working-class speakers versus middle-class speakers. To some extent this can be found in the key characteristics of UK working-class speech such as a tendency to regular use of the 'glottal stop', the 'non-rhotic' dropping of the 'r' or the type of 'homophonization' seen in 'h'-dropping at the start of words. But for Bourdieu an identifiable 'regional accent' takes on its sociological significance as a function of struggles over symbolic power between, fundamentally, classes rather than cultural-geographic isoglosses. The essential structure of the linguistic field is thus hierarchical with its premium poles taken by the dominant social class which institutes its dialect as the standard or 'received' form of pronunciation.

However, such relations are subject to change in the 'market' (Bourdieu and Thompson 1991: 37) where social differences in spoken discourse are subject to variation in 'value'. The linguistic field is not static and varies historically and in quite dynamic ways. This can be seen in relation to the rise of 'estuary English' in the UK where upper-middle-class codes underlying Received Pronunciation have varied and fallen somewhat in social esteem. The rise of 'mockney' (or 'Standard Southern British' – SSB), a conscious assumption of a watered-down working-class east London accent and some of its colloquialisms, is referred to in this report:

> The Queen no longer speaks the Queen's English. Instead she has, along with millions of her subjects picked up the glottal stops and flattened vowels of 'estuary English'. According to Professor Harrington, the monarch has moved away from the plummy, received pronunciation of the 50s, and headed instead for the mockney tones of the lower reaches of our national hierarchy. Forget the way she still says 'orf' for 'off'. Note instead her tendency to pronounce the 'l' in milk as a vowel. (*The Guardian*, 21 December 2000)

This report notes the potential within a language for there to be 'vowel-shifts' in the standard accent (or received pronunciation) in the face of popular social or other forces. The influence of the media, particularly TV celebrities, in the popularization of 'estuary English' as well as its appeal to the new middle classes in Britain (associated with their key political representatives, New Labour, and the articulation of this type of accent in Tony Blair's speeches) shows change can occur in the social status of once subordinated accents or dialects even if, as in this case, it may be stimulated by populist impulses.

Bourdieu states that television is a medium that continues the implicit symbolic violence in language and the 'tacit complicity' between victims and agents (Bourdieu 1998: 17) associated with it. Quite regularly the acting profession, intrinsically concerned with accent and voice as part of its job in portraying character, prompt political concerns about the media's role in stereotyping. Michael

Caine's 2000 Bafta acceptance speech (for lifetime achievement) gave him an opportunity to express his frustration because:

> As a south Londoner with a 'duff accent' he felt ignored and unloved, like 'a stranger in my own country and profession'. (*The Guardian*, 14 April 2000)

Similarly the British actor Ray Winstone's London 'cocky' accent is noted here as:

> if reading from a text in which every T and H has been Tipp-Exed out. Middle D's have gone awol ('di'n'e', 'shoul'n't'). The odd M goes missing too, and all the consonants are mere ghosts of themselves. Written phonetically, his version of 'something' would be 'sa'i'. (*The Times*, 21 August 1999)

Besides the assumption of social inferiority of the cockney accent, this report also assumes that phonetic spelling is value-free. However, as we have noted the principles and the sounds designated to particular symbols/characters in dictionaries and grammars are historically and socially arbitrary. Indeed, the form of 'mirror' representation of linguistic difference in this quote is challenged by more critical writers (e.g. in the essays of the Scottish writer Tom Leonard (Leonard 1995)) because of its ideological role in marking a particular language community.

But when thinking of language and the media the essentially *relational* nature of linguistic meaning is central. Ray Winstone provided the voice-over in a recent television advertisement for the Volkswagen 'Caddymax' car. Generally speaking, in the UK Winstone's cockney accent is associated with the working class and is therefore subordinate in the linguistic field. This is compounded in the particularity of Winstone's voice, whose male form of 'non-rhotic' pronunciation also substitutes 'w' for 'r'. Stereotypically this generally serves to signify in the media male characters of poor education, the working class, and small-time criminals. However, it has also brought Winstone considerable economic gain in film roles depicting working-class life (*Nil by Mouth*) or criminality (Winstone starred in the early 1970s drama *Scum* about young men in a 'Borstal' or young offenders unit) and in this instance his voice has economic value because it helps associate the Caddymax, actually quite a small or even 'feminine' car, with masculinity in a way that might appeal to the white working-class male market. In other words, the symbolic value of any particular accent or dialect in the linguistic field has to be measured in relational terms, *and* in the context of its function or deployment, which in this case is the field of mass media and journalism.

Thus, using Bourdieu prompts us to see how accent, dialect and voice are important 'stakes' in the media as well as in the linguistic field more generally. For example, Don Castellaneta, the voice of Homer in the *Simpsons* cartoon series, reportedly gets paid around $400,000 an episode. However, in 1999 there was a dispute between Castellaneta and Fox, the distributors of the programme, because Castellaneta had used Homer's voice in a CD recording of a political comedy show by the American satirist Paul Krassner which was seen by Fox as contrary to its intellectual property. Similarly, certain voices are also established as those that command authority – for example those contained in pre-recorded Tannoy announcements at train stations:

> It speaks with authority, possibly even with culture. It doesn't try to ingratiate itself with the public by glottal stops, or droppin' the g off the end of a word, like some prime ministers I could mention. But nor does it have the authority born of years of command, evoking the heyday of Empire. (*The Guardian*, 24 August 2000)

It is useful here to draw on historical linguistics studies of standardization in Britain and America (although 'Standard American' is not usually associated with any one particular class group as RP is in Britain). Bourdieu makes a distinction between the 'internal' and 'external' markets in which the former is where the more technical issues of language are at stake, and in the latter more popular issues figure. In the internal market the standards of language are subject to 'scientific' scrutiny by the 'technical corps' of the linguistic field. The external market in turn puts 'technical' issues in linguistics under wider public scrutiny, and then educationists and certainly journalists and other agents credentialized to comment on language in the media become involved. Eighteenth-century Britain was a key period of struggle in the internal market, marked by rising concerns to institute elocution lessons and codify standards of spoken language in pronunciation dictionaries. The concern of these lexicographers and phoneticians, who, as Crowley points out, thought of themselves as scientists, was actually with instituting the English of the educated 'average southern Englishman, when speaking carefully in lecture-room, pulpit, stage or platform' (Crowley 2003: 124). So debates in the internal market need to be followed through into the external market and it is the media that will often popularize concerns about standards. Significant discursive changes in the field of print media, for example the rise of 'Gonzo' journalism in the 1970s, are thus likely to indicate the presence of new social forces that have 'agents' engaged in key intellectual debates on language in the internal field.

In the UK more recently, demands for standardization have figured widely in the media and journalism (Humphreys 2005; Truss and Timmons 2006). These demands for control and standardization of the language are also found in the regular, often annual, production of style manuals, pronunciation guides, or more famously in John Reith's BBC 'language unit', and in both national public service broadcasters and commercial ones. The mass media is now the main site where linguistic standards are reflected upon, perhaps more regularly than in the academy and certainly with more impact socially. In the period following the First World War the BBC was as much concerned about the 'state of the language' as grammarians who were busy producing usage guides (Fowler's in 1926 and Gowers's in 1948).

A similar trend occurred in the USA as NBC began to set pronunciation standards in the mid-to-late 1940s (Bender 1951). NBC felt concerned to institute 'General American' as the key accent of its announcers to meet with what they felt to be the increasingly critical standards of its listeners:

> Thus the standard of pronunciation for the American broadcaster is reasonably based on the speech heard and used by the radio audience that the broadcaster reaches. This means that the broadcaster would use the pronunciation that is spoken by the educated people of the area served by the station. Otherwise he might run the risk of being difficult to comprehend or alienating the approval of the audience. (Bender 1951: ix)

This concern of the NBC handbook with standardizing its 'voice' is historically congruent with Gouldner's theory of how 'careful critical discourse' (Gouldner 1979) started to mark the rising prominence of the new middle classes of this period. A similar congruence is probably going on with the coincidence of the rise in 'estuary English', New Labour, and new cultural intermediaries occurring in Britain in the 1990s. Similarly, in the late 1970s, as the UK adopted a post-Fordist economic model, 'meta-linguistic' concerns also started to figure in the media. This can be seen in the 1979 debate over the news reader William Hardcastle's rather idiosyncratic style of news presentation. Hardcastle was depicted as being 'an anti-speech merchant' in a short essay by Alver Lidell in *The Listener* (at the time the BBC's weekly radio magazine) and following a handful of readers' letters the issue developed over the next year. This resulted in a BBC public report in which academics from the field of linguistics and editors debated the issue and in which Lidell called for an ideal reader who would speak 'educated southern English without affectations or mannerisms or defects, and reading accurately and impersonally' (Burchfield et al. 1979: 5).

Bourdieu's idea of symbolic violence in relation to language therefore places as central historical processes of institutionalization of any particular socially 'arbitrary' accent or dialect – the forces standardizing spoken and written language. This process makes subordinated groups like the working class today feel 'intimidated' and stigmatized (Bourdieu and Thompson 1991: 52) by norms of speech and written language which do not match their own – they experience diglossia. Diglossia is an aspect, often 'misrecognized' by the victims of symbolic power in language, that creates a situation where the standard language can 'only be acquired through special education' (Irvine 1989: 256) such as elocution lessons. The self-censorship and symbolic violence that is experienced by the working class is usually intensified in education (Willis 1972) and other more formal contexts where the standards of appropriateness have been set by the dominant, standard, 'idiolect' of, usually, the middle classes. There is also a strong link between the 'tension' a subordinate language group feels in spoken language and the likelihood of mistakes in written discourse. As historical linguistics shows, spelling is likely to be based on the phonetics of the dominant idiolect which makes subordinate groups victims of 'lexical attrition' (Beal 2006: 55) when their 'voice' becomes undermined.

Socially aspiring subordinate language groups may attempt to mimic or defer to the dominant idiolect. Bourdieu calls this 'cultural good will' and suggests that 'hypercorrection' in grammar and writing or 'hyperdialecticism' (Auer and Hinskins 2005: 356) in the speech of subordinate groups are other aspects of this (Bourdieu and

Thompson 1991: 85–7). Such forms of deference are a consequence of 'misrecognition' of the social and historical 'arbitrariness' of standard forms. In relation to the media, this idea informs Bourdieu's points on the established formality of the language characterizing television interviews in France. He notes in this way how the actual context of the TV interview is set not really by the studio, but by the social and linguistic fields that determine how well or badly people of different backgrounds will 'perform' there:

> Intonation counts, as do all manner of other things. Much of what we reveal is beyond our conscious control [...] There are so many registers of human expression, even on the level of words alone – if you keep pronunciation under control, then it's grammar that goes down the tubes, and so on – that no one, not even the most self-controlled individual, can master everything, unless obviously playing a role or using terribly stilted language. (Bourdieu 1998: 31–2)

The working-class struggles against the forces of standardization because of the intensity of linguistic socialization that patterns the 'habitus'. For Bourdieu the linguistic habitus acts as a constraint – it is not easily abandoned in media or any other contexts. This is more so in spoken language; as Trudgill notes, the phenomenon of encroaching approximation of the vocabulary and spelling of written English in the USA and UK is unlikely to be found in spoken language because:

> Pronouncing our native dialect is something we all learn how to do very early in life, and it is a very complex business indeed, involving the acquisition of deeply automatic processes which require movements of a millimetre accuracy and microsecond synchronization of our lips, jaw, tongue, soft palate and vocal cords. (Trudgill 1990: 11)

Bourdieu's concept of habitus, and particularly 'linguistic habitus', serves to remind us of the embodied nature of language. This means that linguistic value is not subject totally to context, or to the determinations of the market, but also to the type of 'orchestrating' located in the habitus:

> Languages exist only in the practical state, i.e., in the form of so many linguistic habituses which are at least partially orchestrated,

and of the oral productions of these habituses. (Bourdieu and Thompson 1991: 46)

As we have seen, in Bourdieu's view, every 'speech act' derives from the intersection of the class habitus and the linguistic market and these are two relatively independent forces:

> Every speech act and, more generally, every action, is a conjuncture, an encounter between independent causal series. On the one hand, there are the socially constructed dispositions of the linguistic habitus, which imply a certain propensity to speak and to say determinate things (the expressive interest) and a certain capacity to speak, which involves both the linguistic capacity to generate an infinite number of grammatically correct discourses, and the social capacity to use this competence adequately in a determinate situation. On the other hand, there are the structures of the linguistic market, which impose themselves as a system of specific sanctions and censorship. (Bourdieu and Thompson 1991: 37–8)

Bourdieu argues that the 'expressive interest' is indexical, depending on context, but the 'social capacity' to speak is drawn from the class habitus which is more structured but nevertheless has transposability and flexibility.

Chapter 5 on photojournalism shows how social differences in embodiment act in a similar way to accents or dialects in terms of designating variations in non-verbal expression. But such paralinguistic elements accompanying or substituting for spoken language occur also in written forms since any particular orientation to textual forms will be influenced by one's relaxed or tense relationship to the phonetic codes that have dictated pronunciation or spelling and grammar. As Hanks comments, the social field is the key source of linguistic meaning when expressed via Bourdieu's concept of habitus because:

> From a language perspective, habitus corresponds to the social formation of speakers, including the disposition to use language in certain ways, to evaluate it according to socially instilled values, to embody expression in gesture, posture, and speech production. (Hanks 2005: 72)

This point serves to mark the intrinsically social nature of Bourdieu's theory of linguistic competence in contrast to Chomsky's idea that language has a biological location or 'deep grammar', or in contrast to structuralist linguistics' prioritizing of the 'langue' as the source of linguistic meaning. In Bourdieu's approach, the social, embodied and 'stylistically marked' nature of language in action, in 'parole', is crucial for the social analysis of language (Bourdieu and Thompson 1991: 39), but the habitus and the social field are the source of deep 'generative' structures in language 'in action'.

This chapter has only briefly introduced some of Bourdieu's key ideas in his sociology of language and served to relate them to the media. Bourdieu's ideas about language, his focus on spoken language and 'parole', the importance of accent and other oral and paralinguistic aspects of speech, the relational nature of linguistic meaning, and the idea of symbolic violence have only been sketched in here and will be elaborated in theoretical terms in Chapters 2 and 3. Chapter 2 now starts this process by examining how Bourdieu's ideas have been developed by other writers in the field of media studies.

2
Bourdieu, Language and Media Studies

As noted in the introduction to this book, there have been few book-length studies of how Bourdieu's ideas might be applied to the media, and none which looks specifically at language and the media. In fact, it is only relatively recently that Bourdieu's ideas have been elaborated in studies dedicated to the media, many of these taking for granted that the brief statement of his position on journalism (Bourdieu 1998) is the natural starting point to apply his ideas. The following pages argue that the nature of symbolic power in language hardly gets a mention in these studies of the media. Essentially, these studies displace questions of language and the symbolic with Bourdieu's idea of the media as a 'field', as a space of positions which has to be mapped as a pattern of internal relations. So Bourdieu's understanding of the particularly symbolic nature of symbolic power becomes lost as the distinctive textual nature of media practices becomes subordinated to a focus on institutional aspects of the media, the loci of high or low positions ('repositories') of symbolic power at various points of the field. By following the idea of the field alone these studies lapse into a type of sociological formalism, more descriptive than analytical, of the nature of social relations within the boundaries of the media field. Without accounting for language or the symbolic, genre and more generally discursive factors, we cannot give a full account of the media field.

Primary amongst recent Bourdieusian studies of the media has been Benson and Neveu's study of the journalistic field. Although Benson and Neveu note the need for a language focus in media studies, which they suggest should be located mid-way between field and reception studies (Benson and Neveu 2005: 209), this is not actually achieved in their study. Benson and Neveu note a lack of guidance from Bourdieu in terms of analysing the media – they, correctly, see *On Television and Journalism* as being a political rather than a full theory (Benson and Neveu 2005: 198). However, they refer to Bourdieu's criticisms of the 'asociological' nature of the Frankfurt School (Bourdieu and Passeron 1963) as a key early text. They also note Bourdieu's particular use of Saussure (Benson and Neveu 2005: 3) but, characteristically, without any awareness of the major debates in linguistics that this involved him in (on this see Chapter 3).

At this point we should look in detail at Bourdieu's own essay (2005: 29–47) contained in Benson and Neveu's collection because, along with *On Television and Journalism*, Benson and Neveu tend to follow Bourdieu's ideas to the letter in organizing the principles for editing their book. *On Television and Journalism* was a consciously popular text and Benson and Neveu note its status as a 'provocation'. However, Bourdieu notes the 'reality effect' of television discourse in shaping other areas of experience in modern society, although seeing it as having little autonomy in the discursive sense (Bourdieu 1998: 36–7). But in Benson and Neveu's book Bourdieu concentrates on the relationship of the field of journalism to those of the state and economy, claiming that journalism is contained by the state field and also increasingly it is being penetrated by populist, economistic, forces. It is this latter thesis that has suggested that the nature of journalism as a profession should be a key focus (see Matheson, below) because it is under increasing pressure to lower its ethical standards (Bourdieu 2005: 43). In turn, however, populist logics driving journalistic discourse are starting to penetrate the autonomy of other fields, such as science and academia (Bourdieu 2005: 33–7, 41).

These ideas from Bourdieu act as the organizing theses for most of the chapters of Benson and Neveu's book. Bourdieu hardly touches on issues of language in his 2005 essay, or in his book *On Television*, although his richly suggestive concepts of 'taxonomies', tacitly held 'schemes of classification' in journalists' views of the world are suggestive for further research (Bourdieu 2005: 37) but still to be taken up. Bourdieu tends to displace a pluralistic sense of 'schemes of classification' and the symbolic nature of journalistic practices, to the more singular 'logic of the field' (Bourdieu 2005: 39), perhaps due to his concern in his final works with political economy and neo-liberalism. This is what probably accounts for Benson and Neveu, and others in this collection, focusing too heavily on 'field forces' whilst the symbolic 'side' of the principles of 'vision and division', which must also be an aspect of these forces, becomes lost. Thus textual features of developments in populist journalism, its nature as discourse, becomes lost. Admittedly at one point Bourdieu argues that weekly papers in France are indistinguishable due to economic, 'heteronymous', pressures (Bourdieu 2005: 44). However, the idea that we might need to deploy concepts developed in his earlier work to look at the specific textual aspects of such publications to assess whether this is actually a correct thesis (for example, the political weeklies in the UK, *The Spectator* and *The New Statesman*, are very different, not so much in topics, or market, as in discursive and symbolic 'textures') is not posited.

Because of an over-concern with the field side of journalism initiated by Bourdieu, Benson and Neveu themselves never really convey just what the particular 'capital', or stake, is that characterizes the field, preferring to concentrate on depicting certain 'levels' of the field, its national and 'mezzo' ones in particular (Benson and Neveu 2005: 11) or its key institutions (Benson and Neveu 2005: 17). This produces hypotheses which seem to suggest concrete research (which they see as one of the key benefits of the field approach – to stimulate alternative ways of looking at the media) but often feel very abstract indeed:

> Influences emerging from the semi-autonomous journalistic field – a mezzo level organizational, professional, and ideological space – represent an additional variable not previously considered. (Benson and Neveu 2005: 17)

They suggest that economic capital is a 'heteronymous' one in the field but are not really sure what its 'autonomous' capital is (Benson and Neveu 2005: 3–4). Following Bourdieu more or less to the letter of his book on journalism, they see the field as 'weakly autonomous' (Bourdieu 2005: 33) but that it shares a similar stake to that of the political field – to 'impose the legitimate vision of the world' upon its subjects (Bourdieu 2005: 40). The book also notes that Bourdieu is concerned with the way the populist press (often referred to by him as 'omnibus' papers – i.e. tabloids) now 'infects' other fields, such as academia, with its generally lower standards of discourse.

Thus Patrick Champagne in an examination of media coverage of a contaminated blood scandal found that in reaction to it scientists wanted to:

> keep journalists away from its own internal standards and control its members' careers by maintaining a monopoly of consecration. (Champagne and Marchetti 2005: 117)

This focus on the profession aspects of journalism tends to lead the analysis to an over-concern with regulation of the profession, such as monitoring of press 'sensationalism', or the role of the 'peer review'. But the specificity of journalism as a form of linguistic discourse, as both spoken and written practice, is heavily neglected, attention being directed instead to how journalism as a profession relates to the twin forces of state and market. So although Benson and Neveu's book underlines how Bourdieu's approach 'turns' on two metaphors of field and symbol, the latter insofar as it specifically includes language is neglected.

In contrast, Loïc Wacquant's 2005 edited book *Pierre Bourdieu and Democratic Politics* (Wacquant and Bourdieu 2005) is a collection which ranges over topics concerned with the role of political engagement and the public sphere. This book assesses Bourdieu's ideas in relation to Habermas's theory of communication and the public sphere. As Habermas's sociology has been associated with questions of discourse ethics this could have initiated a comparison with Bourdieu's own theory of symbolic power (but see Chapter 4 of this book), a topic that Bourdieu has referred to in interviews in the collection *In Other Words*. However, like Benson and Neveu, Wacquant's study concentrates on the concept of the field rather than symbolic power and language, and thus misses the vital role that language plays in the constitution of political power (what Bourdieu refers to as the 'mystery of the ministry' or institutionalization). Thus whilst referring briefly to Bourdieu's 'sociological pragmatics', and 'modalities of political expression' (Wacquant and Bourdieu 2005: 15), the linguistic aspects of these concepts *as* discourse, which might help us to understand political rhetoric and 'spin', get lost. Even where language seems to be addressed, for example in Champagne's study of opinion polls and 'making the people speak', the specific nature of the language of polls in the press is neglected. Champagne prefers to focus at the mid-range, at the transmission of political discourse by journalists and their role in the interpretation and transmission of the statistical results of polling. Chapter 7 of this book, on opinion polls and the media, in contrast, demonstrates that focusing on the language of polls enhances our understanding of polling as a distinctive form of symbolic violence.

This failure to address the specific 'force' of language in these two major books on Bourdieu and the media is offset by a number of interesting studies and research papers on the media. But some of these feel, as in Benson and Neveu, the need to draw attention to the professional codes of journalism, or to outline more details about the major distinctions within the profession. For example, Marlière points out that Bourdieu has too 'undifferentiated a view' of journalists, attributing 'unified beliefs to its members as well as missing how developments like political party spin doctors might be influencing journalistic production' (Marlière 1998: 223). Elsewhere Marlière, again essentially following *field*-led principles of research, questions whether the idea of 'field' actually aids research in media studies. Like Benson and Neveu, he notes Bourdieu's thesis of the media undermining the autonomy of the 'intellectual field' (Marlière 2000: 203) but he looks at historical trends, some of which seem to contradict Bourdieu's assumptions, such as the supposed trend to an increasing depoliticization of print journalism (Marlière 2000: 201). Marlière notes the critical reaction in France to Bourdieu's 'stigmatization' of journalists, but also stresses some of the normative aspects of Bourdieu's views on journalism, for example his hope to:

> make journalists explicitly aware of the 'perverse structural mechanisms' which instrumentalize them, so that they can react against them more effectively than they do at present. (Marlière 2000: 210)

Chapters 4 and 5 below, on print journalism and photojournalism, elaborate some of the underlying normative ideas in Bourdieu's work in order to specify just where he seems to stand in debates on media ethics. In particular, Bourdieu's concern with the journalistic resort to 'over-generalizing vulgates' in their reports concerning working-class areas of urban life is also noted by Marlière in relation to TV coverage which 'tend[s] to create an image of social problems […] which emphasize the "extraordinary", that is violent actions' (Marlière 2000: 210).

In his own individual work Benson has applied Bourdieu's ideas in studies of the cultural contrasts between different national media fields (Benson 2006). Distinguishing himself from Duval's study of the French business press (which looks at journalistic capital), Benson instead looks at reception and readership demographics (Benson 2006: 188). This involves him in examining cultural and other differences in the content and form of journalism and drawing 'homologies' of how these spaces of production and consumption might be structurally related to one another. Again, the concept of the field dominates Benson's approach and he sees change as more likely to come in the fields from 'external shocks', whilst internal trends in new media like blogs are seen as 'unlikely' to 'transform the class bias of news media'. Benson also argues that the professional codes of journalists are important because they can serve to 'refract' the influence of socio-economic forces. As such, Benson stresses that we cannot just say that journalistic autonomy is in itself a good thing, a key issue for Bourdieu (Benson 2006: 197). Benson refers to Bourdieu's characterization of the discursive content of journalism as always essentially 'euphemistic' in status – because it is fundamentally oriented to its own 'market' rather than the overt news content of the message (Benson 2006: 197) (a point made also by Couldry, below), although he does see the concept of habitus as important in 'research on the distinctive cultural production of columnists' (Benson 2006: 192).

In another study, Benson identifies how the media has autonomy vis-à-vis the political field. Benson's concern here is with the ongoing process of the 'mediatization of politics'. Studying this relationship prompts him to raise questions of 'why some political debates are more or less simplified, personalized, dramatized, or contextualized than others' (Benson 2004: 227). Benson portrays the media as having growing independent effects on politics and society and refers to Klinenberg's study of the way the Chicago media field 'interacted' as a whole to produce a construction of the 1995 heat wave as a 'natural rather than all-too-human disaster' (Benson 2004: 281). But language and journalism is again not addressed here and of the eleven variables that Benson identifies for a thoroughgoing analysis of the media, only one obliquely refers to language, in terms of context and stylistic variables, and this is seen as probably only important in international comparative studies of the media (Benson 2004: 282–3).

However, Schultz in a study of journalistic 'gut feeling' or habitus argues that we need to see journalism as part of the internal field of language. One of the problems of over-stressing the field at the expense of discursive practice is that it is sometimes quite difficult to 'place' journalists in 'the' field of media or journalism. Thus Schultz gives the journalistic field equal status to academic linguistics in terms of linguistic power. She also sees journalists as involved in practices that span a number of fields:

> The journalistic field is part of the field of *cultural production* together with the arts and sciences, a field that is occupied with producing cultural, 'symbolic goods'. Furthermore, the journalistic field is part of the field of *power*, not least because the constant cultural production of social discourse not only implies production of categories for 'vision' of the social world, but at the same time, categories also of 'division', or more simply put: to give a name, is also to place within a hierarchical, symbolic space. (Schultz 2007: 192)

Schultz is concerned with what factors might constitute a 'journalistic habitus', and also like Benson concerned with outlining a number of professional types (Schultz 2007: 194) but this is balanced by looking at the undiscussed ('doxic') principles they espouse (Schultz 2007: 194). But, as with Benson, the profession is the chief focus for understanding the journalistic field, rather than what the language journalists use might reveal about their deployment of symbolic power.

Matheson in his study of journalists' reflections on the professional values of their work also gets us a little closer to language as a topic in its own right. Matheson has a type of postmodern take on Bourdieu, where the 'self-constitutive' role of discourse is stressed (Matheson 2003: 167). He therefore examines journalists' views of their use of language and notes that they hold a 'one-to-one' view of the relationship of words to reality. They also adopt ideas of 'transparency and immediacy' as key values – they see it as a virtue to translate 'difficult' sources, whilst holding on to ideas of a 'unitary' readership (Matheson 2003: 174–9). In contrast to Benson and Wacquant's stress on the concept of the field, Matheson drifts into the quite opposite mistake – seeing the journalistic field as one made up of textual distinctions, or a discursive order alone. Matheson examines the 'meta-discourses' journalists hold in relation to their role as writers but in this and other aspects of his analysis he does not think back to deploying some of the ideas of *Language and Symbolic Power*.

It is probably Couldry's work that has most extensively attempted to link Bourdieu's concern with symbolic power and the field to a comprehensive account of the media. Although not directly concerned with the linguistic dimensions of media texts, his key foci being on 'frames' lying between text and audience, rituals, and on more 'general tendencies' of the media (Couldry 2000: 40), Couldry nevertheless has in theoretical and empirical studies managed to remind media studies of the importance of symbolic power in Bourdieu's approach:

> Symbolic power impacts on wider society in an even more pervasive way, because the concentration of society's symbolic resources affects not just what we do, but our ability to *describe* the social itself; it affects the perception of the inequalities in the social world, including the unequal distribution of those very symbolic resources themselves. (Couldry 2003c: 39)

In this respect, Couldry sees the media as key to the 'habitus' of modern societies (Couldry and Curran 2003: 42) and argues in his essay on 'media meta-capital' that a 'return' to Bourdieu's theory of symbolic power has benefits missing from the later developments in the field approach (Couldry 2003a). This refocusing on the specificity of the media as a field in its own right and, more importantly, with its own form of capital, would enable media theory to express the extent of its impact on other fields and stop some of the confusion about just where the boundaries of the field lie in relation to the state and economy, or cultural field. Thus Couldry argues that:

> We might, in the long term, see 'media capital' in its own right as a new 'fundamental species of capital', in Bourdieu's phrase, that works as a 'trump card' in all fields. (Couldry 2003a)

In other studies, Couldry sees this as legitimated due to the:

> overall result of countless process of reproduction in talk, belief, and action, both by media producers and media consumers. (Couldry 2000: 39)

Couldry argues that for Bourdieu language and discursive practices must be understood in relation to the *unsaid* – to the doxiac and social, which are often 'euphemized' by the seeming autonomy of language (Couldry 2005).

The third key theme of this book is to expand Bourdieu's sociology of language to take account of lay forms of reflexivity. Couldry is also critical of Bourdieu in this way, noting the failure in *The Weight of the World* to reproduce lay accounts in a more faithful sociolinguistic manner. Couldry also argues that Bourdieu failed to consider the media's role in *creating* social and cognitive distinctions, rather than in just reflecting them. He notes that work on the media in *The Weight of the World* suggests a concern to counter media news accounts with those of lay narratives and, in a world of 'blogging', this could well become easier. This concern marks Couldry's other work on the way media coverage of protests is at odds with protesters' views and how the latter are able to 'de-naturalize' media frames (Couldry 2000: 150). Couldry, there-fore, wants to give space for the potentiality of lay actors to be reflexive about the media.

To summarize, on the whole these studies have elaborated the soci-ological side of Bourdieu's field approach. But nearly all of the above works, which are somewhere close to the concerns of this book, have nevertheless neglected the symbolic, parole, side of Bourdieu's analysis of language and how the media is a particularly discursive form of practice. Without this we have only a partial understanding of the media's role as a major locus of symbolic power. In contrast, this book's aim is to show that we can use Bourdieu not just to understand the social structural side of the field of media, but also its functioning as a specific form of symbolic practice. Using Bourdieu to analyse the language of the media allows us to understand what is significant about it in terms of its distinctiveness as a social practice. Thus, by keeping the media in focus as 'textual' practice, but also where appropriate framing it by field analysis, we can avoid taking over unproblematically the categories of 'vision and division' of actors involved there. Looking at the media field in discursive terms, then, allows a 'break' with the 'illusios' that have currency in the journalistic field and to 'construct the object' of the media as a topic of analysis and further our understanding of the particularity of its form of 'capital' and symbolic power.

3
Interrogating Bourdieu on Language: Critical Discourse Analysis, Postmodernism and Ethnomethodology

This chapter engages with some of the key criticisms of Bourdieu's approach in the field of linguistics and discourse analysis and then moves on to discuss rejoinders and modifications of his position. Bourdieu has been criticized from traditions within linguistics, such as structuralism and critical discourse analysis, and from directly competing sociological approaches to language, such as sociolinguistics and ethnomethodology. We will look, firstly, at critical discourse analysis and postmodernist approaches and then go on to consider, principally, the ethnomethodological challenge to Bourdieu. The discussion in this chapter is focused on the theoretical issues that Bourdieu deals with in *Language and Symbolic Power* and the repercussions of his criticisms of sociolinguistic approaches and what he refers to as 'subjectivist' approaches, such as interactionism and ethnomethodology. As such, the theoretical issues here relate to academic debates in the 'internal' area of the linguistic field. As will become apparent, it is these important theoretical issues that have been left unaddressed by the literature which has applied Bourdieu's ideas to the media. These debates are very much theoretical ones and abstract, but they nevertheless form the background to the arguments in the chapters which discuss language and the media in case study form.

Critical discourse analysis and postmodernism

One of the more elaborated engagements with Bourdieu's approach to language has been by Ruqaiya Hasan. Hasan is a key exponent of 'systemic functional semantics' (SFL), an approach developed from

Halliday's work (Halliday 1985) which focuses on how meaning is generated in language. Some of the key concepts of Halliday's work, such as 'linguistic register' and 'dialect' have similarities to the relationship between field and habitus in Bourdieu's approach. A theoretical engagement between these types of approaches could enable an enrichment of our understanding of the class and language relationship. But, in coming from the field of linguistics, it is a characteristic of SFL that it finds Saussure a key forebear to producing a semantic-focused account of language. Hasan is, therefore, critical of Bourdieu's reading of Saussure because it is 'limited' (Hasan 1999b: 29), over-stresses the 'arbitrary' aspect of language and misses 'Saussure's further comments on the value and identity of the linguistic sign' (Hasan 1999b: 447). Bourdieu focuses on language at the level of practice, parole and how this reveals underlying structural relations of symbolic power. Due to this, Hasan argues that Bourdieu misses the relatively autonomous nature of language in discursive practices – its independent causal effects. Hasan also attributes to Bourdieu a 'naming theory of meaning' (Hasan 1999b: 48), suggesting that he over-socializes language so that the established 'semiotic' and grammatical 'formalism of the word' (Hasan 1999b: 53) is overlooked. The outcome of all this is that the semantic and established meaning of words, the grammatical functionality and overall 'facticity' of language, is neglected by Bourdieu, and as a result he loses the 'meaning aspect of language' (Hasan 1999b: 57–8).

Hasan's criticisms originate from the very principles of the linguistic field that Bourdieu set out to contest and therefore it is obvious that Bourdieu will be called to account for concentrating on the 'secondary' level of language. But Hasan also argues that Bourdieu fails to consider language as a force in the social shaping of the habitus. Hasan argues Bourdieu has to leave this out of his account because to include it would reveal his over-dependency on the 'secondary', parole, relations of language (Hasan 1999b: 67). Hasan agrees that Bourdieu's concern with language as parole allows him to establish a sociological view of language that subordinates the non-arbitrariness of linguistic, semantic, meaning in order to stress the causality of symbolic power. Hasan thus argues that Bourdieu's approach 'implicates only the phonological signifier, whose relationship to context, meaning and wording is never constitutive but simply one of expression' (Hasan 1999b: 63).

The critical discourse analysis (CDA) of Chouliaraki and Fairclough shares many of the SFL assumptions of Hasan. However, they also underline how critical discourse analysis wishes to avoid the overly 'structuralist' or 'objectivist' side of Bourdieu's account. Like Hasan, these writers criticize Bourdieu for excluding how language can be constitutive of social relations (Chouliaraki and Fairclough 1999b: 400) rather than always being secondary to them. So by missing this specific force of language to be constitutive of social life, Bourdieu must therefore fail to account for how linguistic capital is itself part of classificatory struggles (Chouliaraki and Fairclough 1999b: 401) – its particular role in the very constitution of the self or the habitus (Chouliaraki and Fairclough 1999b: 402). These writers argue, therefore, that Bourdieu needs to have a theory of language which can account for its distinctive 'force' (Chouliaraki and Fairclough 1999b: 402), which recognizes its own 'orders' that act as an independent source of variation in meaning (Chouliaraki and Fairclough 1999b: 403). So, in contrast to Bourdieu, CDA gladly admits to being 'textually-oriented' (Fairclough 2003: 2) and that its approach to social forces via a post-structuralist Foucauldian conception of 'orders of discourse' is a more comprehensive theoretical way to link discursive orders and social orders.

Chouliaraki and Fairclough's (1999a) more extended theoretical statement of CDA makes a number of other points against Bourdieu. In many areas the writers admit to drawing on elements of Bourdieu's 'constructionist-structuralism', particularly his view that there is a need to engage with this 'depth science' of the 'generative mechanisms' of practices (Chouliaraki and Fairclough 1999a: 30). In contrast to postmodern accounts, they argue that Bourdieu is important in showing the social constraints on the natural propensity of language to 'hybridity'. However, they argue that in totally 'subordinating' language to social forces Bourdieu cannot produce a more dialectical form of explanation:

> Bourdieu articulates the power of discourse to constitute the social only as a power of certain social groups in certain circumstances. In not recognizing that discourse is inherently constitutive of social life, Bourdieu slips into an objectivist ontology which posits a dimension of the social that is outside the ongoing process signification [sic] and constitution [...] CDA by contrast develops

a theoretical practice which is simultaneously oriented to the analysis of communicative events (a hermeneutic task of interpretation) and the analysis of their structural conditions of possibility and structural effects. (Chouliaraki and Fairclough 1999a: 30)

Chouliaraki and Fairclough go on to argue that Bourdieu's approach fails to account for the specificity of 'contemporary forms of mediation, such as television, or any institutional complex or field with its own structural logic and forms of capital' (Chouliaraki and Fairclough 1999a: 103). Additionally they charge Bourdieu with inadequately explaining how linguistic capital is constituted by such things as the ability to access its more highly valued stylistic features (Chouliaraki and Fairclough 1999a: 102). They suggest this is the result of Bourdieu's reduction of symbolic struggle to 'people acting with the single motive of accumulating capital'. Chouliaraki and Fairclough thus argue that the principles of linking the two areas of concern are not clear in Bourdieu's work:

> This is important in order to disentangle the two views of struggle that remain unresolved in Bourdieu's work: classificatory struggles; and struggles for profit [...] In focussing on symbolic struggle as struggle for *access* to legitimated capital ('objective' rhetorical styles [...]), Bourdieu essentially plays down the crucial issue that linguistic capital *per se*, in the form of discourse as representations of social processes and relations, is part of the struggle for the constitution and classification of social (field) relations. This is to neglect on Bourdieu's part of what we referred to [...] as the 'content' of the fields. (Chouliaraki and Fairclough 1999a: 104)

In this view, Bourdieu can only account for changes in language, such as the rise of 'Mockney' (see Chapter 1) if there is a corresponding change in social structure. We have seen that the burden of Bourdieu's account is to argue that what occurs 'in' institutions concerned with discursive practices, such as the media, must be related to the social forces that structure the linguistic field, such as the state and economy. But this does not necessarily imply that the other fields do not also mediate these forces – by the 'field effect'. Chouliaraki and Fairclough admit that Bourdieu's approach can account for the 'content' and the specificities of the media as a distinctive field of discursive practice, even though social forces, such as neo-liberalism, predominate in his account. In fact, Bourdieu's idea of the fields prompts linguistic analysis to pursue how the discursive 'content' of a number of fields may be 'homologous' as a result of social forces located in the power fields:

> Interdiscursive analysis is a key dimension of analysis of field relations which can foreground the potential for social change in the complexity and hybridity of late modern forms of practice, something that Bourdieu has been accused of neglecting ...
> (Chouliaraki and Fairclough 1999a: 115)

But there is still a fundamental divergence, which centres here on how to understand textual *practice*. CDA's fundamental concern is with *textual* orders rather than orders of *practice*. Bourdieu's key concern is to explain how textual practices relate to social structural forces so language is necessarily secondary to these as a form of practice, although it can still be seen as both resource and medium of social-symbolic struggles. CDA diverges from this, constituted by an approach which is always predicated on the belief that the vital structure of language is language, rather than language as a realization of social practice.

In contrast, Bourdieu's approach has the *merit* of presenting a clear explanation of the nature of the social forces that influence language and underlie 'performativity'. The drawback of the 'dialectical' aspect of CDA is that it tends to give a sociologically vacuous, textually focused analysis or privileging of the type of meta-discourses which Foucault called 'serious speech' (Foucault et al. 1972), for example psychoanalytic discourses. But, by following Bourdieu, parole itself can be considered as 'serious', that in the case of radio (in Chapter 6) 'intonation counts', and the powerful influence of the spoken word in everyday interaction and in the media suggests that the separation of the 'serious' and 'simple' is tenuous and cannot be coherently maintained (which Chapter 8 argues is an aspect of text messaging). Chapter 5 on photojournalism also shows in this context why Bourdieu's ideas also generate criticisms of Barthes's semiology that are similar to those articulated here against CDA. Bourdieu is fundamentally critical of the type of 'semiotic vision of the world' (Callewaert 2006: 80–1) characterizing the type of

Foucauldian ideas underlying CDA, and Roland Barthes's semiology itself. Fundamentally, Bourdieu insists that discourse cannot explain discourse (Callewaert 2006: 77) and that practice only has meaning in practice (Ledeneva 1995: 9), sociological 'rules' or principles that contrast his approach to the privileging of texts in CDA.

There have also been internal criticisms and Bourdieusian developments within CDA which point to its own weaknesses. Scollon's (2001) work revises some of the principles of CDA and in doing so stresses the role of the habitus and early socialization in influencing symbolic practices. Also influenced by Vygotskian 'psychology of mediated action', Scollon in this way examines the 'ontogenesis' of practice and follows the implications of different patterns of socialization of children for explaining variations in the way they engage in symbolic practices. Scollon maintains a grasp on Bourdieu's conceptualization of a 'homologous habitus' (Scollon 2001: 37) and the implications of ontological 'non-reversibility' that Bakhtin (and Bourdieu) sees in practice. Scollon's 'unit of analysis' is not therefore 'discourse' and text, but the process of mediation of these (Scollon 2001: 3). This maintains a hold on Bourdieu's view of 'action in real time as related to the reproduction of social structures' (Scollon 2001: 9). So Scollon draws back from the SFL and Foucauldian principles underlying CDA, and instead understands practice as arising in the 'contingencies in life, rather than its larger levels' (Scollon 2001: 22).

Postmodernism

At a number of points in this book it is noted how postmodern approaches to language and the media give much more scope to textual aspects of media practices than Bourdieu. In Chapter 8 on text messaging in particular, an engagement with postmodern ideas on mobile technology is developed. At this point, however, there is a need to address Butler's arguments about Bourdieu's understanding of 'performativity' in language (Butler 1997). Butler, like Bourdieu, is often considered to be a post-structuralist, but her understanding of subjectivity and the autonomy of discursive structures makes her, in fact, much closer to the postmodern position. The postmodern position on language, however, is not so much an underlying rearguard defence of linguistics as a source of analysis of media practices, as in

CDA, but more the result of a propensity of this approach to insist on the need to 'de-differentiate' texts and the social.

One of the key issues in this encounter is over the interpretation of the nature of embodiment in language practices. As mentioned in Chapter 1 in relation to Chomsky, Bourdieu's view of the embodied nature of language is not a biological-determinist one. Also, for Bourdieu, the body is inscribed fundamentally by social practices, rather than inscribed by singularly discursive ones. Butler's position on reflexivity in language is the key interpretation of Bourdieu's ideas on the performative and one which stresses his concern with embodiment. But she extends the idea of embodiment of language in a way that significantly departs from Bourdieu. Butler argues that Bourdieu's concern with language and embodiment is undermined by his subordination of language to social forces. For Butler, like Chouliaraki and Fairclough, language itself is constitutive of the body and is, therefore, an essential part of agents' ability to be reflexive in discursive practices, and more generally to monitor their behaviour.

In his approach to peformativity, Bourdieu differentiates himself from Austin (1975) who sees it as depending on linguistic conventions that enable contextually based authority relations (Butler 1997: 147). Austin gives as an example how an individual's right to name a ship is the result of contextually designated and legitimated conditions (e.g. ceremony or pageant) that help to give the utterance its 'effect'. Austin points out that this is the only way to identify this type of statement as being distinct from the ability of any other speaker to use similar words. Bourdieu argues that beyond the features of a setting the ultimate and socially significant conditions for felicity 'lies in the mystery of the ministry' (Bourdieu and Thompson 1991: 75) which endows an individual utterance with such authority in the first place, rather than any particular contextual circumstances *per se*. Bourdieu admired Austin's work and argued that his criticisms were 'aimed at formalist readings which have reduced Austin's socio-logical indications ... to analyses of pure logic' (Bourdieu 1990b: 29).

So, Bourdieu defines performativity as *socially* instituted symbolic power, and claims that high social and political 'capital' will give the agent the 'right to name' and to be recognized as having the right to name. Butler argues, in contrast, that due to this Bourdieu has a 'mimetic' view of the relationship of linguistic habitus and field, claiming instead that there is an ambivalence at the heart of all social norms (Adkins and Skeggs 2004: 206). To support this argument, Butler draws on Derrida's criticisms of Austin's view of performativity, and by implication Bourdieu's own account of symbolic power as the key factor in structuring the conditions for 'felicity':

> Derrida argues that the breaking of an utterance from prior established contexts constitutes the 'force' of an utterance. (Butler 1997: 141)

Thus, where Bourdieu sees the body as norm-governed, and discursive practice and performativity as primarily subordinate to the larger social-shaping of the linguistic field (for example by neo-liberalism), Butler sees the body as much more intransigent and likely to be the source of 'confounding' of norms (Butler 1997: 142). This gives Butler the scope to see performativity as arising *in* discourse, part of the inevitably reflexive nature of language in practice. The generative aspects of the habitus, its ability to be 'deployed' in a wide variety of ways according to contexts, but always within 'limits' of its linguistic capacities, is for Butler a key locus of agency. Commenting on Butler's view, Lovell thus argues that Bourdieu loses touch with this in his understanding of language as practice because he 'reduces the power of words to the power of social institutions' (Lovell 2004: 3) and also because he disconnects language from embodied performance:

> Speech acts are not 'merely linguistic' but also bodily, and Butler identified therefore the possibility of discordance between what is spoken and what the body says [...] It is in the margins, between what is said in words and the eloquence of the body, that resistance, even subversion may be nourished. And, secondly, because the social norms and institutions depend for their production on iteration and reiteration in performance, there is a 'logic of iterability' that makes even the most entrenched institutional norms vulnerable to a subversion and transformation through transgressive performances. (Lovell 2004: 4)

As Chapter 5 on photojournalism will argue, Bourdieu nevertheless allows us to see how bodily demeanour only really takes its meaning, is understandable, if we contextualize its 'displays' in relation to the conditioning factor of symbolic power. And, as Lovell herself shows in her elaboration of Butler's example of Rosa Park's Montgomery bus protest, the larger context (the political field in this case) had to be right for Park's protest to be 'felicitous', however individually reflexive she might have appeared to be.

Bourdieu's approach, therefore, has been skewed here by Butler on the basis of postmodernist principles to suggest that class, race and gender are the product of 'naming' (Lovell 2004: 10). But, it is possible to articulate these criticisms somewhat differently, to give them more resonance in relation to Bourdieu's approach. This idea will be developed below where Bourdieu's ideas will be related to understanding agency and reflexivity in language by drawing on Bakhtin's ideas of 'polyphony' and cultural understandings of identity in language found in the concept of 'voice'. These concepts can help to maintain the specificity of Bourdieu's focus on language and symbolic power whilst enabling his approach to account for the forms of embodied reflexivity in discourse that Butler identified.

Developing Bourdieu: phenomenology and ethnomethodology

Many of the criticisms of Bourdieu in CDA and postmodernism come down to saying that, as a sociologist, Bourdieu is more concerned with social structure and its reproduction than with social change. However, there are resources in Bourdieu's work which actually contradict such charges. For example, Bourdieu coins the concept of 'hiatus effect' to explain how a once stable relationship between the education field and the middle class was disrupted as a result of social trends, lower-class fractions entering the field and 'devaluing' particular subject areas, in the process that led to the Paris events of 1968 (Bourdieu 1990a). In this section I argue that the criticisms coming from CDA and postmodernism can be addressed by re-stressing the phenomenological aspects of Bourdieu's approach. But in order to do this we need to engage, firstly, with another approach that is criticized by Bourdieu – ethnomethodology (Bourdieu 1977). Ethnomethodology nevertheless offers ideas which can help to develop his ideas in relation to agency in language.

We have seen that, in contrast to Saussure, Bourdieu is critical of the idea of the 'arbitrary' status or nature of the linguistic sign. Bourdieu's position suggests that language is fundamentally in an indexical relationship with the structures of the social system. Irvine explains that by being indexical:

> [C]orrelations between realms of linguistic differentiation and social differentiation are not wholly arbitrary. They bear some relationship to a cultural system of ideas about social relationships, including ideas about history of persons and groups. I do not mean linguistic variation is simply a diagram of some aspect of social differentiation [...] but that there is a dialectic relationship mediated by a culture of language (and of society). (Irvine 1989: 253)

Bourdieu's approach to language assumes it is in an indexical relationship, or secondary, to structural, social, forces. But this does not mean there is always a *direct* determining relationship between social forces and discourse. Bourdieu sees the linguistic field as a semi-autonomous, intervening structure lying between social and political structures. In Chapter 2 we have seen that attempts to apply Bourdieu to the analysis of the media have tended to overplay the field metaphor at the expense of ideas of language and symbolic power in the media. However, in terms of arguments against alternatives to Bourdieu's approach, the concept of field is an important resource in suggesting the nature and locus of the indexical aspects of meaning.

Bourdieu is, however, critical of ethnomethodology for its overemphasis on the routines of conversation and, more importantly, on its view of the indexicality of language, more properly speech acts, because it misses how the class habitus makes linguistic behaviour deployable or transposable. Indexicality is usually associated closely with ethnomethodology (Weider 1974), and is a key concept in explaining how the meaning of 'members' talk is 'situational' (Douglas 1971: 33). This 'occasioned' nature, the contextuality of meaning, contrasts to the structuralist idea of langue and the paradigmatic and synchronic levels of discursive meaning. As Heritage notes, in ethnomethodology rules and norms are always seen as being *realized* and this emphasis helps us to understand the particularity or the 'whatness' of an interactional situation (Heritage 1984: 109). But Bourdieu has criticized the unsociological nature of indexicality in the following way:

> Thus, when we speak of class habitus, we are insisting, against all forms of the occasionalist illusion which consists in directly

relating practices to properties inscribed in the situation, that 'interpersonal' relations are never, except in appearance, *individual-to-individual* relationships and that the truth of the interaction is never entirely constrained in the interaction. This is what social psychology and interactionism or ethnomethodology forget when, reducing the objective structure of the relationship between the assembled individuals to the conjunctural structure of their interaction in a particular situation and group, they seem to explain everything ... in terms of the experimentally controlled characteristics of the situation. (Bourdieu 1977: 81)

Due to its interpretation of indexicality, ethnomethodology is uninterested in the constructivist-structuralist principles that inform Bourdieu's epistemology, his stress on the need to sociologically construct (rather than simply describe in minute detail) the object of study:

> ... the 'fixation on readily visible orderliness' [...] of ethnomethodologists and the concern to keep the analysis as close to 'concrete reality' as possible which inspires conversational analysis [...] and fuels the 'micro-sociological' intention, can prompt us entirely to miss a 'reality' that escapes immediate intuition because it resides in structures that are transcendent to the interaction they inform. (Bourdieu and Wacquant 1992: 144)

In addition, Bourdieu argues that ethnomethodology tends to make universalizing explanations of linguistic and other forms of social communication (Bourdieu and Wacquant 1992: 73) because of its individualizing focus.

Bourdieu's arguments appear to totally conflict with the ethnomethodological objective of developing concepts to represent members' representations. However, one of the key arguments of ethnomethodology and conversational analysis is that there is a need to demonstrate the influence of social structures. If situations reveal 'demonstrable' or 'indigenous imports of an discursive "event" and of their context *for their participants*' (Schegloff 1997: 183) then structural effects should be focused on, and an attempt made to explain their particularity. The general view of ethnomethodology is that post-structuralists like Bourdieu fail to break with commonsense notions of practice because concepts like the field are too remote from the actual processes that constitute the 'quotidian' (Jalbert 1999: 7). But we can make more comparability between these two positions if we argue that the concept of the field actually has heuristic, rather than ontological, analytical status so that it simply serves to 'open the analyst's eyes to relations which are not simply open to observation or could be thought via intuition' (Bourdieu 2005: 31). In doing this the concept of the field simply directs attention to 'indexical' contexts which ethnomethodology misses, for example, the impact of symbolic power in talk arising from the historical and social determination of paralinguistic features such as accent, dialect and voice.

The ethnomethodological position on language stresses a sense of indexicality in which linguistic meaning is produced in the process of conversational exchange. But Hutchby notes two general directions in ethnomethodology – a concern with 'generic structures' such as 'adjacency pairs' which mark conversational analysis (CA), or Garfinkel's approach which focuses on the 'socially occasioned' character of linguistic meaning (Hutchby 2001: 201). So ethnomethodology can deal with the idea of there being structural factors involved in situated interaction. Hutchby also quotes Schutz's view of practice as having the sense of our being 'continually' making sense of our interaction with others (Hutchby 2001: 49). And ethnomethodologists focus on speaker and addressee in actually quite *abstract* terms because they see these as universal in status. The concepts of habitus and field are, however, similar sociological 'constants' which point attention to how linguistic practice is affected by structure in the 'particular' situations that ethnomethodologists focus on. Bourdieu's sociology directs us to attend to the media as a field, but for ethnomethodologists its particular effects will always be subordinate to the universal, fundamental structures of interaction or conversation which inform 'members' resources' that energize contexts.

Ethnomethodologists also stress how commonsense distinctions, such as that between knowledge and belief, may also influence discursive situations (Jalbert 1999: 87). Journalists and editors are therefore fundamentally engaged in everyday, indeed universal, forms of human communication (Jalbert 1999: 87). Thus, in contrast to media studies approaches (particularly text-focused ones like semiotics), this concern with 'readerly' practices allows them to see how agency might arise in highly structured practices, such as radio conversation (Scannell 1991).

The divergences of ethnomethodology and Bourdieu are at their widest here because ethnomethodology tends to analyse situated, highly localized forms of interaction to ascertain linguistic (or, more generally, *communicative*) meaning. Bourdieu argues that this is the 'occasionalist' fallacy of ethnomethodology, a criticism of their idea of indexicality, because it misses 'a "reality" that escapes immediate intuition because it resides in structures that are transcendent to the interaction they inform' (Bourdieu and Wacquant 1992: 144). It may, therefore, just be possible to relate Bourdieu's concern with the established structures of the linguistic field with that of the ethnomethodologists' concern with 'universal structures', but they could never accept a prioritizing of the distinctive forces of fields of discursive practice, such as the media, as the privileged sources of communicative meaning.

Much of ethnomethodology is, therefore, taken up with abstracted persona in its concern with the universal positions of speaker and addressee (seen, for example, in the preference the approach has for analysing telephone dialogue). This contrast is underlined in relation to the social role of accent in conversation which as far as ethnomethodologists are concerned simply does not count (on this see Chapter 8). Accent and other paralinguistic aspects of language, although highly observable, rarely become 'topics' in the course of discursive interaction or 'thematized' there. Similarly, the concept of field as a means to best *explain* the causation of sociolinguistic practices (rather than to *represent* in realist fashion) is constructionist in status and not likely then to be reflected on in the course of everyday practice. Ethnomethodology's more 'grounded' approach suggests that empirically demonstrable processes, such as 'repairs' in conversation, are the key to a break with common sense – by the generation of a distinctive technical vocabulary to describe it.

Ethnomethodologists do sometimes note that there are structural aspects of language which cut across particular situations, even though they usually see these in universal, even 'primordial' (Boden and Zimmerman 1991: 12–14), terms. Ethnomethodology takes for granted some of its key categories such as 'speaker' and 'addressee', positions which actually need to be theorized. They therefore miss how many social factors intervene in determining how these roles will be assumed, for example the way women tend to give more 'support' in conversation than men (Coates and Cameron 1989). As critical sociolinguists like Coupland show, the meaning of a conversation often turns on the 'accommodation' of one speaker to another's accent (Coupland 2001). In other areas, however, the ethnomethodological approach to language, and the media, shares some of the concerns of Bourdieu's approach. For example, Schegloff's influential critical article on CDA is similar in its arguments to Bourdieu, showing concern to access 'readerly' activities or the 'understandings of the participants' (Schegloff 1997: 180) – the level of parole. Ethnomethodologists also want to avoid a textualist focus (Jalbert 1999: 11), like Bourdieu, although they more strongly assert how agents exhibit active, reflexive, behaviour in discursive practices.

An uncommon link: Husserl's phenomenology

But, at a more fundamental theoretical or philosophical level, Bourdieu's approach has similarities to ethnomethodology, particularly in relation to the work of Husserl. Much of Bourdieu's sociology is infused with principally Husserlian phenomenological concepts. Amongst these are the contrasts he uses between 'doxa' and reflexivity, 'protension' and 'project', and the concept of habitus, and the idea that scientists must make a 'second break' and return to consider their ideas in relation to ordinary practice or commonsense (Bourdieu 1977, 2000). Ethnomethodologists also draw on Husserl's criticisms of common sense infiltrating into scientific analysis. They regard Husserl's concern with 'intentionality' in practice as important in opening up the constant process of monitoring that goes on in language and other practices. But ethnomethodologists miss how Husserl's philosophy always saw 'intentionality reaching down to the most basic forms of recognition [and] beyond subjective to cultural and more sophisticated forms of experience' (Keller 1999: 2), just the areas of 'structure' that Bourdieu is concerned with.

Jalbert's study of the media from an ethnomethodological approach, argues that intentionality is 'unthematized' (Jalbert 1999: 14) in alternative accounts of the media. Jalbert contrasts the ethnomethodologists' concern with 'intentionality' and 'motive' to the over-stressing of the 'force of objective structures' in sociological approaches (Jalbert 1999: 10) like Bourdieu's. In this sense ethnomethodologists are more open to revealing not just the way 'members' create meaning and orderliness in textual practices, but also how fragile the establishment of meaning can be. Social practices have, then, 'an ever present reflexive potential, or "criticability" if they are to be maintained or "carry on"' (Jalbert 1999: 39). The influence of Husserl's ideas in ethnomethodology also motivates its concern to account for lay forms of reflexivity in everyday discursive practices.

Bourdieu also draws on Husserl in his counterpoising of doxa and common sense to intentionality or what Husserl, when referring to scientific forms of reflexivity, calls 'predictiveness'. In contrast, ethnomethodologists look to how both sides of this equation have common grounds in intentionality, which they see Husserl as maintaining as fundamental to all practices. In this way ethnomethodologists recognize the argument, contained in Husserl's *Experience and Judgement*, of seeing a number of 'levels' of intentionality between reflexivity and common sense or doxa. Thus Husserl argues that common sense rests on a bedrock of 'protodoxa' – an idea which is similar to ethnomethodology's concern with the 'default options' in language (Boden and Zimmerman 1991: 7–8), or the deep levels of determinacy of language (Schegloff 1997: 183). For Bourdieu, in contrast, protodoxa indicates the fundamental elements of communication which are beyond context or indexicality – the 'taken-for-granted', standardized forms of language established by past symbolic struggles in the linguistic field (Myles 2004).

It is, however, important to bring these two interpretations closer together because both stray one side or the other of the structure–agency problem. The ethnomethodologists' insistence on the ordinariness of 'intentionality' and the 'motivated' character of speech can also be related, in this context, to another aspect of Husserl's thinking – how we move from low states of intentionality, from 'protention' (intuitiveness) to more active states or 'predictiveness' (being more fully conscious of our actions and of the situation). There are similarities here because Bourdieu regularly makes use of these ides but in order to assess how very *different* this project is from the intuitiveness of practice:

> Husserl did indeed clearly establish that the *project* as a conscious aiming at the future in its reality as a contingent future must not be conflated with *protention*, a pre-reflexive aiming at a forth-coming

which offers itself as quasi-present in the visible, like the hidden faces of a cube, that is, with same belief status (the same doxic modality) as what is directly perceived; and that is only when it is retrieved in scholastic reflection that it can appear, retrospectively, as a project, which is not in practice. (Bourdieu 2000: 208)

The area where these contrasting interpretations might come together is in the idea of there being an intervening state of awareness identified by Husserl as *Zuwedung* – a looking forward or toward objects in the perceptual field (Husserl et al. 1973: 55–6) and situated between the states of 'project' and 'protention'. It is in this sense that Husserl always insisted that science or 'pre-predictiveness', must revisit its roots in common sense or doxa. This was not, however, only in order to avoid the error of reproducing commonsense, but also to remind science of its origins, as human, social, practice. As Derrida comments on Husserl's *Origins of Geometry*, even scientific concepts are for Husserl *être-objets* (Derrida et al. 1978: 27), that is they are produced in a particular 'form of life'. Ethnomethodologists interpret this Husserlian distinction as a key epistemological safeguard, a warning to keep from taking over commonsensical 'members' resources' in sociological explanation, seen, for example, in the regrounding of the study of language and the media in terms of its interactional role (Jalbert 1999). In contrast, Bourdieu argues in his idea of the 'second break' that this means there is a need to guard against the 'intellectualist fallacy' which attributes to common practice the reflexivity of science (Bourdieu and Eagleton 1999).

However, Bourdieu's interpretation of Husserl is nevertheless important for modifying ethnomethodology where he argues on Husserlian principles that sciences like linguistics are implicated in social domination because, although they may have broken with common sense, their technological sophistication obscures a very socially abstracted, individuated, form of 'scientific' inquiry. This is also the basis of the criticism Bourdieu makes against the 'spokespersons', for example – journalists – who 'deal in' language and make themselves:

The exclusive agents of the ontological leap presupposed by the move from *praxis* to *logos*, from practical sense to discourse, from practical vision to representation, that is, access to the order of specifically political opinion. (Bourdieu 2000: 185)

Bourdieu's own particular use of Husserl makes him unable to see how lay actors might emerge from 'doxa' because of the determining power of the linguistic field, for example, which works to circumscribe the anarchic potentiality of language to break out of its various forms of control – for example its 'technicization' by the media, political rhetoricians and spin doctors.

But Bourdieu is recognizing here that there is a potentiality in lay forms of reflection to break out of dominating doxa, just as the ethomethodologists stress intentionality with this purpose in mind. However, he is also concerned to note that just being able to grasp the arbitrariness of symbolic power does not mean that the alternatives may not still be misperceived:

> The dominated, whose interests are bound up with the raising of consciousness, i.e. with language, are at the mercy of the discourses that are presented to them; whenever they emerge from doxa they are liable to fall into allodoxia, into all the false recognitions encouraged by the dominant discourse. (Bourdieu 1984: 461)

We must agree with Bourdieu (and Husserl) that lay forms of reflexivity are not scientific, but they are nevertheless an essential element in discursive practices and yet that the ethnomethodologists are right to stress accounting for 'intentionality' as an important aspect of everyday language practice. The problem is that this is not always available to direct observation, the preferred method of ethnomethodology. For example, it is often the case that the 'dominated' do reflect on their experience of 'self-censorship' and class stigmatization in language. In this respect, Goffman's concern with the sociological significance of 'self-talk' notes just how such lay mental reflection arises in more or less dialectical reciprocation to the injuries we experience in language as a result of symbolic power:

> We kibitz our own understandings, rehearse or relive a run in with someone, speak to ourselves judgementally about our doings [...] and verbally mark junctures in our physical doings. (Goffman 1981: 79)

Goffman actually refers to Bourdieu's work in this piece in relation to the problem of the stigmatization of local accents and dialects, and the media's role in intensifying this. He also sees this as intimately linked to the process of standardization in the linguistic field where 'national standards of appropriateness' and:

> [N]ational schooling and media-inspired sophistication have given such faults a coercive force in which populations, in the sense that almost anyone breaching the standards in question can be made to feel ashamed for having done so. (Goffman 1981: 210)

As Chapter 4 argues, Bourdieu fears that journalists have a propensity to act against lay 'ways of seeing the world' (Bourdieu 1998: 19–22) whilst Chapter 5 on photojournalism argues that this struggle is not limited to words but also to images, as photojournalists apply their own technical visual vocabularies to 'frame' their subjects. But, as other chapters of this book show, lay people can be critically aware of being subject to the symbolic power of the media, of having their ways of seeing the world, and being seen, manipulated (Chapters 6 and 8).

Bakhtin and 'voice'

Another source from which Bourdieu's account could be rebalanced is in the concept of 'voice', an idea which is also developed in Chapter 6. We have noted that Chouliaraki and Fairclough argue that Bourdieu fails to grasp the particular determinations that arise from the semantic content of language due to his focus on class, field and parole. In this view, when the stakes in discursive struggle are reduced simply to those of symbolic capital, then the meaningfulness of conversational exchanges, what they refer to as the quality of 'voice', becomes diminished. It is for this reason that Chouliaraki and Fairclough prefer Bernstein who they suggest maintains a grasp on voice as message as much as voice as accent and style:

> In the voice-message dialectic Bernstein locates a possibility for social change that is absent from Bourdieu's work [...] In Bourdieu, classification (the positioning of voices) is the primary site of contradiction and struggle, and message is just the arbitrary realization of voice [...] For Bernstein, on the contrary, if contradictions and dilemmas are suppressed in voice, they emerge in the process of interaction, in message, as sources for a 'yet-to-be-voiced', for

alternative discourse, other subject relations of power. (Chouliaraki and Fairclough 1999a: 112)

In contrast, Bourdieu sees elements of voice, such as accent, as para-linguistic, as socially marking language and take on their meaning along with other socially determined factors like dress and bodily demeanour (Bourdieu and Thompson 1991: 70).

But voice can direct us to consider how language itself often becomes thematized, or a reflexive form of linguistic activity in lay discursive practices. Writers who have developed this aspect in a more sociological way have turned to Bakhtin's theory of 'polyvocality' and there are a number of points where Bakhtin's stress on 'language as living dialogue' (Bakhtin and Holquist 1981: xv) relates well to Bourdieu's approach. In particular, Bakhtin notes that any individual's speech is filled by degrees of 'others' words' which may have particu-larly socially 'evaluative tones'. This idea has affinity with symbolic violence and 'lexical attrition' in Bourdieu's account of symbolic power and 'cultural goodwill' or complicity. But Bakhtin also stresses agency in spoken language and how people can 'assimilate, rework, and reaccentuate' the words of the dominant (Bakhtin and Holquist 1981: 89). In this respect thinking in terms of its possible *stylization*, or how the dominant language can be redeployed due to the 'hybridity' of speech, allows us to recognize how lay actors can experience reflex-ivity in discursive situations. This can be seen as an aspect of the more tacit understandings of 'appropriateness' (Bourdieu and Thompson 1991: 78) recognized by Bourdieu as well as in the idea of intentional-ity in ethnomethodology.

Guilianotti (2005) refers to Bourdieu's view that the working classes tend to internalize their subordinate position in terms of symbolic power (vis-à-vis the standard language). However, he uses Bakhtin's concept of 'polyvocality' (Guilianotti 2005: 34–3) to rec-ognize how the 'performativity' associated with voice is common in subordinated language communities:

Bourdieu's theories regarding cultural distinction and human agency imply that the voices and broader cultural habitus of dom-inated groups are oriented towards 'practical' ends rather than more aesthetic or expressive forms of self-fulfilment. Alternat-ively, I would suggest that the stratified models of Bernstein and

Bourdieu underplay the polyvocality of social agents moving between and across linguistic codes or habituses respectively. (Guilianotti
2005: 324)

Guilianotti contrasts this quality in voice to the tendency of the
mass media to 'commingle voices'. The concept of voice thus helps
Guilianotti to identify how subordinate language communities create
more positive or 'phatic' forms of social recognition in the media – a
process he calls 'vernacularization' (Guilianotti 2005: 344) of media
messages. Thus voice points to the possibility of more 'readerly' and
reflexive appropriation of the language of the media by lay actors,
and develops a Bourdieusian perspective on language to address
issues of lay reflexivity.

From sociolinguistics, Coupland (2001) also draws on Bakhtinian
ideas of voice and argues that subordinate language communities use
dialect and accent to maintain 'phatic' contact. Like Guilianotti he
recognizes how the media may offer a space for the 'stylization' of
voice. Coupland argues that there is a need to avoid the sociolinguists'
'commitment to authentic speech' and to focus on the performative
and playful aspects of dialect and mediated forms of stylization of
accent (Coupland 2008). Similarly, sociolinguistic 'accommodation
theory' suggests that class prestige and power are important factors
influencing stylistic shifts in accent in ongoing conversational
exchanges between speakers (Giles et al. 1991). In a study of stylization in radio presenters' discourse, Coupland notes how they 'playfully
and actively select from a pre-existing repertoires of culturally significant dialect forms of English to project shifting social personas and
stances' (Coupland 2001: 347). The cueing, reflexive and 'mannered'
nature of such frame shifts, variations in announcers' pronunciation,
all suggest that authenticity of accent and dialect are subject to recon-
figuration and 'local practices of enacting and reconstituting culture'
are a form of 'entextualization' (Coupland 2001: 369).

Conclusion

The concept of voice alongside an elaboration of Husserlian ideas
related to intentionality can, therefore, help to address some of the
problems in Bourdieu's sociology of language pointed to by postmodernist, CDA and ethnomethodological approaches. This is not to

move Bourdieu away totally from the position on language he adopts in *Language and Symbolic Power* – constructionist-structuralism – but to rebalance the 'subjectivist' and 'objectivist' polarities of his sociology. The essential focus of Bourdieu's approach to language is the key role given to the social field in the order of determination – it has 'epigenetic' status. Questions of the historical institution of the middle classes' linguistic habitus in the linguistic field due to stand-ardization are rarely addressed in CDA, postmodernist and ethno-methodological approaches. Such concerns are shied away from because of fears of reductionism or, even – as a result of a kind of naïve complicity in this process – their failure to properly construct the object of analysis. Bourdieu's approach keeps the social in focus rather than following the logic of texts, and in doing so we are less likely to fall into the error of the over-exorbitization of texts in post-modernism or over-technicized accounts such as in sociolinguistics. Nevertheless, it is also important to avoid over-stressing doxa and complicity in agents' (particularly working-class agents') experience of symbolic violence and the media – and recognizing the Husserlian grounds of Bourdieu's ideas is a means to achieve this.

Part II Case Studies

4
Journalism, Language and the City

This chapter analyses how urban regeneration stories are reported in the evening press. As we noted in the introduction, Bourdieu does not go deeply into the nature of journalistic discourse in his key book on the media, *On Television*. However, at various other points in his work, particularly in some of the essays contained in *Political Interventions*, the nature of journalistic discourse is more directly addressed. In particular, Bourdieu coins the concept of 'paralogism' as one means by which we might be able to identify how journalistic discourse is complicit in the imposition of symbolic violence. But in many more of these 'interventions' Bourdieu gives other partially formulated ideas about the political and linguistic dimensions of journalism which can be usefully deployed to extend his arguments on language into this field.

Questions relating to the reporting of urban regeneration and development are highly politically charged in contemporary society, and therefore are an important area of media analysis. Bourdieu himself directly recognized this when he addressed the relationship between the 'intellectual and the city' with reference to Husserl's concern that the intellectual should try to act as a 'functionary of humanity' (Bourdieu et al. 2008: 207). Bourdieu's concern with Husserlian ideas about the relationship between scientific and lay forms of language and reasoning introduced in Chapter 3, is therefore again referred to in this chapter as a means to criticize contemporary developments in the reporting of urban regeneration issues, since the press is concerned to report the 'technical' issues of regeneration to a largely lay readership.

The politics of the city press have become increasingly significant in recent years as George Monbiot notes:

> For many years the local press has been one of Britain's most potent threats to democracy, championing the overdog, mis-representing democratic choices, defending business, the police and local elites from those who seem to challenge them. (*The Guardian*, 10 November 2009)

Examining journalistic discourse in this area thus evokes important issues of 'spatial' rights and justice and this chapter engages with this topic in the context of the political and social debates on the role of regional print media. For a long time ideas of public communication, the public sphere, urban justice or 'rights to the city' have been dominated by Habermasian approaches (Forester 1993; Merrifield and Swyngedouw 1997). In Chapter 2 it was noted that an engagement between Habermas's ideas on language and political communication and Bourdieu's might prove fruitful. In this chapter this idea is developed by examining how Bourdieu's ideas on the political role of journalism, both in analytical and prescriptive terms, provides an alternative source to address these issues. We will see that Bourdieu's arguments on the ethics of journalistic practice provide a sociological form of understanding of performativity that contrasts to the ethico-philosophical reasoning characterizing Habermasian approaches (Habermas et al. 2004).

Journalistic discourse and neo-liberalism in planning and urban regeneration

Since the 1990s in the UK the role of the media and journalism has been enhanced in the process of planning and urban regeneration. City press journalism has moved beyond straightforward reporting, or comment, on these issues to a much greater *involvement* in them. In the immediate post-war years in the UK, a fairly rigid planning 'regime' placed the emphasis on regional, local and city governing authorities to initiate public consultation. Planning was a highly bureaucratized process carried out under the sway of local authorities and city council planning offices. But now the power of these essentially governmental-bureaucratic locations of planning has been reduced and pluralized by the entrance into the field of a far greater number of quasi-governmental agencies, many of which are situated in the private corporate sector. Healey (1995: 257) notes that in the 1990s the 'penetration of the vocabulary of economic evaluation into public policy formation and implementation' produced an instrumentalist 'technical methodology' and 'management by performance criteria' as planning increasingly became dominated by neo-liberal political ideology. Healey noted that the trend to 'partnerships' between local government, central government regional agencies, and private contractors in urban planning reduced local government planning departments' control of the planning process (Healey 1995: 267), in effect further eroding democratic accountability in planning.

It is in this context that the city press and media's role in planning has been enhanced as it increasingly takes over the role of communicating planning issues to the wider public. There are arguments that having the city press assume this role is preferable to the situation where planning debates and consultation were restricted to 'draughty' town hall rooms where the public was effectively debarred by the slow and ponderous nature of the process. But these newer developments can be criticized because they have brought conditions in Britain much closer to those described in Logan and Molotch's critical analysis of 'urban fortunes' in the USA (Logan and Molotch 1987). Logan and Molotch found there that the city press and media were very important in the process of 'boosting' cities. They note that city newspapers and journalists get involved in urban regeneration for a number of pragmatic and ideological reasons that take them well beyond their traditional reporting function. Democratic accountability then becomes an issue where journalists who regularly cover planning and urban regeneration become involved with, or influenced by, members of 'urban growth coalitions'. Urban growth coalitions are networks of bankers, property developers and architects who work to promote the image of the city in order to attract inward investment. It is often the case that coalitions form, or inspire, 'flagship' regeneration projects that may not always be economically sound, at least in terms of benefiting the majority of the city's population (as seen below in relation to Article 1, see Figure 1). For pragmatic reasons the city press and media also depend upon the economic prosperity of their city bases, and therefore are motivated to become active in planning debates, not just in terms of reporting and comment, but by actually stimulating interest and conducting consultation exercises and public debates.

This enhanced role of the media and press in planning and consultation means that journalistic discourses raise questions of the democratic role, function and accountability of city press print journalism. Given that journalists have now had to take on this role how are they adopting it? What expectations do they and others have of 'urban journalism'? What attitudes to the public do journalists hold? What characterizes journalistic discourses on urban life and its governance and development? These questions are pursued in this chapter by textual analysis of urban regeneration reports and articles and by relating these to the political and sociological issues relating to city journalism and its impact on the public sphere.

Bourdieu, journalism and textual analysis

The examples discussed in this section represent news reports on urban regeneration and development collected from a UK city evening newspaper during a period of six months. The corpus contains 142 reports of all types (including features) of which 72 appeared in the news section, 8 were comment columns, 10 diary (social), 25 features (of which 5 were letters pages), and the remaining 27 appeared in the business pages. The average word length of the reports was 370 (including headlines along with subheaders) and reports below this word length were excluded from the corpus. The newspaper was a tabloid, so the average report's total text generally took up around a quarter of the page space. However, the reports as a whole usually take up more space than this because all but two of them contained one or more photographs or illustrations (such as architects' drawings). The actual ratio of photographs to reports can be assessed in relation to the analysis in Chapter 5 where 69 reports contained photographs. Features and letters pages usually took an entire page with word counts of around 850 or 14 column inches, whilst comment columns were of around 280 words (the letters pages that were included were ones where there were significant exchanges on an urban regeneration issue).

Characteristically, one of Bourdieu's key concerns in the analysis of journalistic discourse is to underline its role in social classification.

We saw in Chapter 2 that Bourdieu has met with criticism because of his negative views of journalists. But Bourdieu is critical of journalists because he sees them as needing to be much more professionally self-critical/reflexive in their work. He therefore sees the press as too prone to adopting ideas that have been established as 'common sense' as a result of, primarily, neo-liberal discourse and 'newsspeak' (Bourdieu and Wacquant 2001). Bourdieu thus sees a key failing of the press being its resort to the use of 'over-generalizing vulgates', a type of populist intermediation of neo-liberal economics or other 'technical' forms of discourses:

> You read on the front page of *Le Nouvel Observateur* about 'the return of sentiment' [...] These media coups are symbolic *coups de force* that are struck in all innocence, and all the more effective for being unconscious. There is a sense in which this can only be done because the people who practise this violence are themselves victims of the violence that they practise, and this is where we get the false science of the half-educated that likes to give the appearance of scientific ratification to the intuitions of common sense. (Bourdieu et al. 2008: 70)

This idea of vulgarization is important because it suggest that, when concerned with representing urban issues, journalists are likely to be swayed by similarly 'technical' arguments. Due to the pervasiveness of neo-liberalist discourses in regeneration today, planners act as 'primary definers' of urban discourse and are likely to be the key sources for journalists. As such, their views are likely to be adopted by journalists in preference to lay sources, on the assumption that they have the technical and, probably, cultural acumen to prioritize their 'right to opinion'.

Bourdieu argues that because journalists are concerned with mass audiences or readerships, they therefore also should be more reflexive in their use of language. If they were so, then it would be more likely that they could then work to stimulate debate and include more of the opinion of publics usually excluded from these kinds of debates:

> A number of words that we use without even thinking about them [...] are categories of perception, principles of vision and division that are historically transmitted and social produced and

reproduced, principles that organize our perception of the social world, and especially of conflicts; and political struggle essentially aims at maintaining or transforming these principles, reinforcing or changing our view of the social world. Journalists therefore play a central role, because among the producers of discourse it is they who wield the most powerful means for circulating and imposing these. They thus occupy a privileged position in the symbolic struggle to make things seen and believed. (Bourdieu et al. 2008: 323)

In terms of debates about the city press, journalists are therefore likely to assume the dominant ideas, the depictions, classifications and prescriptions of powerful 'primary definers' such as planners, businesses and other elites in the growth coalition. But this is not so much a result of a direct conspiracy with members of an urban growth coalition, but more due to the way in which they use language unreflexively. Journalists are also less likely to give credence to lay and alternative (such as local pressure groups') discourses because they are not recognized as compelling, technically or rationally. Wahl-Jorgensen, for example, has found that editors regularly dismiss lay forms of argumentation (as revealed in letters to the editor) in a derogatory fashion as the 'idiom of insanity' (Wahl-Jorgensen 2007: 156).

Paralogism

Bourdieu thus coins the idea of 'paralogism' to identify the way in which journalistic discourse encodes unstated assumptions about the social order. In other words, it is one aspect of the vulgarizing of the language in journalism:

When someone says 'The king of France is bald', two senses of the verb 'to be' are involved, and an existential proposition (there is a king of France) is hidden by a predictive statement (the king of France has the property of being bald). Attention is attracted to the fact that the king is bald, while in reality, the idea that there is a king of France is smuggled in as self-evident. (Bourdieu et al. 2008: 322)

Paralogism in journalistic discourse suggests the need to refer back to Bourdieu's more general criticisms of language. We need to see journalistic discourse in light of its limits, the historicity of its classificatory principles. Analysing the text of press reports on the city is, then, both an analytical and prescriptive task because in revealing its 'false universalisms', its propensity to use 'over-generalizing vulgates' and 'paralogism', we can point to how symbolic violence in the planning process is projected in the press and, by implication, how it might be avoided.

As Bourdieu notes, much of what counts as 'paralogism' is dependent upon variations in the tense of the verb 'to be'. One might say that really all variations in discourse are dependent in this way! But by being aware of this it is possible to become more critically aware of the way the language of the reports works to either confirm or put into doubt the status of a regeneration project or issue. One consequence arising as a result of focusing on this variable is that the speech (or reported speech) of different sources also significantly varies in relation to it.

Article 1 (Figure 1) is an example of paralogism appearing in one of the opinion articles. This piece was triggered in response to comments by a local bishop who had criticized high-profile redevelopment projects that had little relevance for the socially excluded and unemployed. The piece describes the impact of the tower on the city's skyline and then the nature of the bishop's criticisms. By paragraph 5 the article starts to hint that a non-technical opinion coming from a bishop might be suspect ('Now you can question'). But the article moves to reporting a number of facts and figures which hardly seem to square with any idea that the press might be working consistently to boost its home city. However, it is significant that when the report moves to comment, and from description to proposal, its argument reveals paralogistic assumptions:

For local government, opportunities for large-scale ... interventions are few and far between. That is why the council – and indeed the M.E.N. [*Manchester Evening News*] – took the morally difficult decision to back plans for Britain's first supercasino.

It wasn't that they, and we, were unaware of the possibility of creating 'problem gambling' in areas that could least afford it. It was that the need for 3,000 low-skilled jobs [...] was such that the risk was one worth taking.

Figure 1 'Monument to modernity is a symbol of division' (*Manchester Evening News*, 21 July 2009, p. 8, Opinion)

The underlying 'existential' assumption here is that, no matter what its form, and here it really is of the most morally suspect type, any type of economic investment is a good thing. The burden of the piece is to subordinate the (paradoxically!) 'lay' view of the bishop and the evidence of social inequality in the city to the logic of the market. This article, therefore, indicates how journalists seem to find it hard to escape the use of the undeclared logics of paralogism in regeneration debates, the assumption of the legitimacy of 'technical news sources' and the close involvement of the city press in urban regeneration and planning.

Secondly, although at first sight the bishop's comments about regeneration are deemed correct, the piece undermines this by its assumption that it is only the free economy that can make a difference:

> It wasn't that they, and we, were unaware of the possibility of creating 'problem gambling' in areas that could least afford it. It was that the need for 3,000 low-skilled jobs in Beswick was such that the risk was one worth taking. Then Gordon Brown decided he knew better, and took those jobs away.

The underlying assumption of the technical superiority of the market, and stimulating conditions via regeneration projects sympathetic to it, is seen as the more realistic means to address social problems. Thus, whilst this article quotes from a number of statistical and factual sources accounting for the nature of urban deprivation and seems to be sympathetic to the socially excluded, the discursive vulgate of neo-liberalism, here seen (ironically) as manifesting itself as a supercasino, prompts the writer's regret that it was not adopted.

Elsewhere the report depends on a neo-liberal post-municipal-socialist position to sustain its argument:

> 'Sharing the wealth' is one of the council's guiding policies; until the credit crunch struck, unemployment had been falling and rates of educational development creeping up. But their powers to transform inner-city estates simply don't match the scale of the problem.
>
> It was only at the last Budget, for example, that ... Manchester's ... councils were finally told they would be allowed to take

control of providing adults with work-related skills. Until then decisions were taken by quangoes and the government – distant bodies less able to understand what needed to be done, and how.

So what at first seems to be sympathetic to the case for a democratic reinvigoration of city council power is, however, undermined by the piece's only substantial policy suggestion – to allow the market free rein. Making more realistic suggestions lies well beyond the existential horizon of the feature; it is unable to state any tenable alternatives because of the lack of credibility given to the bishop's opinions.

During this debate on regeneration, which ran across the paper's news, comment, features and letters pages, other aspects of journalistic discourse and language in relation to urban regeneration became apparent. The bishop's original comments were made in respect to the appearance of a skyscraper offering 5-star international hotel and leisure facilities, along with duplex private accommodation apartments. This gives some substance to why the tower became a symbol of the increasing social divide that marked the city. Thus Article 2 (Figure 2), a features-diary piece, kicks off with reference to the bishop's original statement about the tower (which, significantly, is reduced to one word, 'dreadful') and, a little lower down, a direct quote which gives the reader some sense of the burden of his words. But the rest of the piece is essentially a series of quotes from an interview with the architect. Significantly, the architect is directly quoted in nearly 25 per cent of the text (21 of a 68 line total). As a diary report, social concerns displace political ones and this genre, in contrast to the comment piece above, allows the architect's own particular voice to come through rather than just that of the journalist's (as in Figure 1). Although this voice is probably unattractive to many, it nevertheless allows a clear position to be articulated within the constraints of the news values marking diary reports (i.e. having a generally entertaining and upbeat tone), but at least how that voice will be received will vary according to the reader's own attitudes because, although clearly espousing the values that the architect's 'high' lifestyle represents, the article is much more polyphonic than the prescriptive comment of the article in Figure 1.

Figure 2 'Ian's sky-high ambition' (*Manchester Evening News*, 20 July 2009, p. 11, Diary)

To be or not to be regenerated

As noted above, paralogism depends heavily on subtle variations in the tense of the verb 'to be'. The ontological status of regeneration and redevelopment projects and the entire notion of 'planning' pitches journalism into the area of what Habermas (see below) would call 'teleological-theoretical' discourse, discourse oriented by its very nature and technical concerns to envisioning the material future of the city. In the following reports, we can see how this tense shifts along a scale between the twin modal auxiliary verbs of 'would' and 'could'.

Article 3. BIRTHPLACE OF FISH AND CHIPS COULD BECOME ASIAN BAZAAR

A historic market place could be turned into an Asian bazaar because of a slump in customers. The market has stood for 150 years and is known locally as the birthplace of fish and chips. But officials say it has fallen on hard times in recent years due to lack of investment.

Article 4. IT'S NOT THE END OF THE ROAD FOR PEAKS BYPASS (reproduced in Figure 3)

A controversial bypass could still go ahead – even though the government has dropped the project. Council bosses have vowed to try to revive the [project] with £100 m of local cash.

Article 5. £650 m PLAN TO REVITALIZE THE HISTORIC HEART OF THE CITY HAS BEEN UNVEILED

A £650 m plan to revitalize the historic heart of the city has been unveiled. Nearly 1,000 new homes would be built in the [...] area – together with two new hotels, shops and offices, and a European style plaza. A new 'commercial quarter' would make the most of the area's closeness to other more prosperous areas of the city.

Article 6. ECO-FRIENDLY VILLAGE TO RISE FROM THE ASHES OF COLLIERY (reproduced in Figure 4)

A former colliery that produced tons of coal for 150 years is to be transformed into a zero-carbon village.

Modal auxiliaries like 'would' and 'could' are more commonly used to refer to *past* events, the past participle indicating reflection on what might have been ('would have/had'). However, it is a peculiar function of paralogism in journalistic discourse on urban regeneration and planning issues that the main sense of these auxiliaries is one that is oriented to the *future*. Generally, 'could (be)' was found to be resorted to more regularly (38 times) than 'would' (23 occurrences) as the key verb in the news reports. 'Would make' in Article 5 seems to indicate

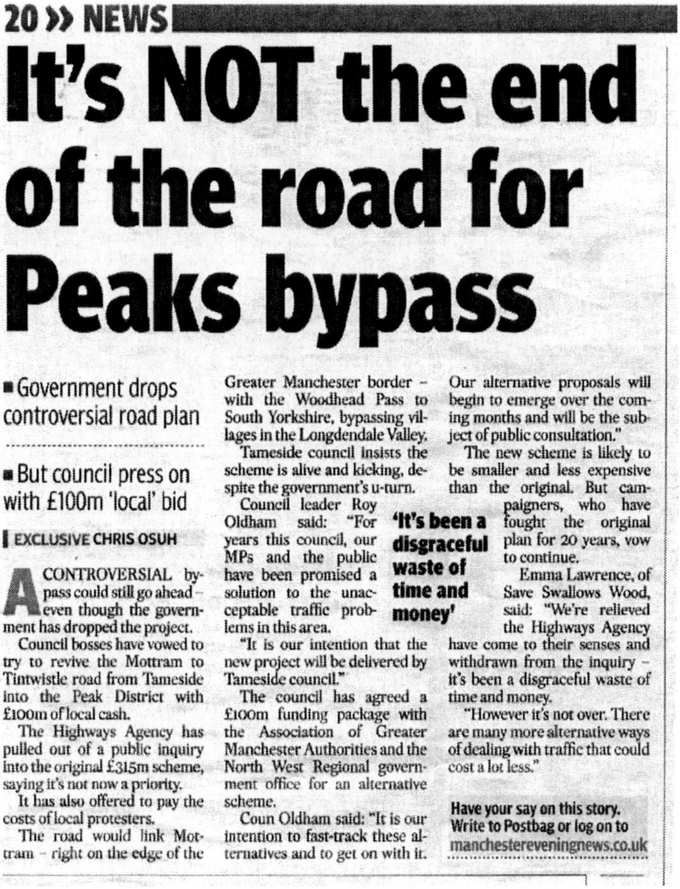

20 >> NEWS

It's NOT the end of the road for Peaks bypass

■ Government drops controversial road plan

■ But council press on with £100m 'local' bid

❚ EXCLUSIVE CHRIS OSUH

A CONTROVERSIAL bypass could still go ahead – even though the government has dropped the project.

Council bosses have vowed to try to revive the Mottram to Tintwistle road from Tameside into the Peak District with £100m of local cash.

The Highways Agency has pulled out of a public inquiry into the original £315m scheme, saying it's not now a priority.

It has also offered to pay the costs of local protesters.

The road would link Mottram – right on the edge of the Greater Manchester border – with the Woodhead Pass to South Yorkshire, bypassing villages in the Longdendale Valley.

Tameside council insists the scheme is alive and kicking, despite the government's u-turn.

Council leader Roy Oldham said: "For years this council, our MPs and the public have been promised a solution to the unacceptable traffic problems in this area.

"It is our intention that the new project will be delivered by Tameside council."

The council has agreed a £100m funding package with the Association of Greater Manchester Authorities and the North West Regional government office for an alternative scheme.

Coun Oldham said: "It is our intention to fast-track these alternatives and to get on with it.

'It's been a disgraceful waste of time and money'

Our alternative proposals will begin to emerge over the coming months and will be the subject of public consultation."

The new scheme is likely to be smaller and less expensive than the original. But campaigners, who have fought the original plan for 20 years, vow to continue.

Emma Lawrence, of Save Swallows Wood, said: "We're relieved the Highways Agency have come to their senses and withdrawn from the inquiry – it's been a disgraceful waste of time and money.

"However it's not over. There are many more alternative ways of dealing with traffic that could cost a lot less."

Have your say on this story. Write to Postbag or log on to manchestereveningnews.co.uk

Figure 3 'It's NOT the end of the road for Peaks bypass' (*Manchester Evening News*, 5 August 2009, p. 20, News)

a stronger sense of possible realization of the plan than 'could', although not as 'perfect' as the full form of 'to be' seen in Article 6 which is in the 'active voice', for the main part, and this makes it seem to confirm the status of the development as going ahead.

But in Figure 3 paralogism is also apparent even when the actual status of the bypass is in doubt ('It is our intention that the new project will be delivered by Thameside council'). This type of paralogism

Figure 4 'Eco-friendly village to rise from the ashes of colliery' (*Manchester Evening News*, 7 August 2009, p. 30)

parallels the example seen in Article 3, another project which is also actually still in development ('the councillor said the proposal was one of a number being considered'). Similarly in Figure 3, the headline describes the project in the *present* tense when it has actually *been* shelved, reinforced this time by the resort to the more conventional auxiliary modal in 'the road would link ... '

Shifts in the tense of the verb 'to be' in these reports are important because they have implications for the attitudes readers will adopt towards the proposals. The shifts from 'could', 'would' and 'is' all actually work in favour of regeneration projects rather than the alternatives, even when the project is at issue or of social concern. The key role of paralogism here, then, is in subtly infusing the reports with the underlying assumption that regeneration is not only in and of itself a 'good thing' but it has preferred ontological status. Thus, where Bourdieu sees paralogism as predicated on assumptions about standing social relations, this variation indicates how it can act to give almost *factual* status to projects that actually are just that – projects oriented to the future – to the 'might be'.

Figure 3 is also an example of journalists' resort to the use of what can be termed a 'compensatory coda', a common rhetorical device in these types of reports. Reports tend to 'compensate' for their assumption of a dominant voice by ending with a quote, the 'last word', to the subordinated voice or opinion apparent in this report. The use of this device means that the reports assume a highly dubious form of 'normalization' of the (actually unequal) social relations that may be, and usually are, at odds in planning debates. The direct quote from a local resident towards the end of this report thus serves to complete and terminate it, and allows an alternative view, for 'balance'. But like all such codas it is subsumed by the generally positive burden of the report (around 75 per cent of the text) in favour of the development. There were very few occurrences, in fact only three, of the compensatory coda not coinciding with paralogism or working in the opposite direction as the result of privileging lay opinions.

Discussion: Habermasian ethics or Bourdieusian sociology in the analysis of urban regeneration reporting?

In this section I want to elaborate on how the context, the 'indexicality' of these reports, relates to broader developments marking the field of urban planning. Planning in capitalist society is in tension between democratic ideas of inclusion of citizens in the urban development decision-making process and the very real material exclusion of ordinary people from it due to private property. What this section argues, then, is that we cannot understand paralogism simply in its textual manifestations – it must also be understood in relation to the field. At the same time, these broader debates about the influence of 'structural' forces can serve to set the context for understanding the contrast between Bourdieu's and Habermas's approaches to discourse and the nature of performativity. Traditionally city planning has met with considerable criticism from the left. Marxist accounts of planning and consultation processes, prior to the changes indicated above, were mainly concerned with how seemingly independent and democratically controlled local and city authorities worked to further the interests of capital. Marxists saw planning as ideologically contradictory because planners consider themselves 'technicians' despite their deep involvement in actually dealing with social issues. Castells and Lebas (1985) saw the profession as functional for capitalism not because it is technically efficient but because it is socially and ideologically effective. In technical terms, planners fail due to their work being inevitably contradicted by the dynamics of the capitalist economy. They nevertheless act as part of the apparatus of the local state's setting out of planning and public consultation as a 'scenario for compromise':

> [A]s an urban political process, planning effectively appears to be a 'place' for negotiations and mediated expressions of the conflicts and tendencies which (according to general social determinations) confront urban organizations, and through it the whole of social and economic organizations. (Castells and Lebas 1978: 84)

This apparent 'social and technical neutrality' of the profession allows it to be effective at two levels:

> [A]t the ideological level in terms of the rationalisation-legitimation of social interests, particularly through planning documents; at the political level, as a privileged instrument of negotiation and mediation which all groups present attempt to appropriate in order to vest themselves with a social and technical neutrality – this of course without planners themselves being able to change things in any way. (Castells and Lebas 1978: 86)

David Harvey, similarly, sees planning as a state apparatus charged with the reproduction of capitalist social relations. To facilitate this ideological role the planning system must be relatively open to democratic inputs whilst its characteristic discourse is instrumental. The 'communicative action' of planning is, to use Habermas's terms, 'systematically distorted' because its democratic function is infused by instrumental knowledge:

> The principle of rationality is an ideal – the central core of a pervasive ideology – which itself depends upon the notion of harmonious processes of social reproduction under capitalism. The limits of the planner's understanding of the world are set by this underlying ideological commitment. (Harvey 1996: 188)

Harvey is, however, concerned to underline the communicative aspects of planning:

> In resorting to tools of repression, co-optation, and integration, the planner requires justification and legitimation, a set of powerful arguments with which to confront warring factional interests and class antagonisms. In striving to affect reconciliation, the planner must perforce resort to the idea of the potentiality for harmonious balance in society. And it is on this fundamental notion of social harmony that the ideology of planning is built. (Harvey 1996: 187)

It is due to this combination of instrumental knowledge and 'systematically distorted' communication that planning discourse works to exclude substantive questions about social justice (Harvey 1996: 191). As we have seen, in the present context press reporting on the planning process imposes similar ideological effects or symbolic violence.

In contrast to these, fairly traditional Marxist approaches, Habermas's theory of 'communicative action' focuses much more on the nature of communication or political debate in the 'public sphere'. In terms of communicative action, Habermas describes how different forms of knowledge associated with applications in the economy and polity ('system') and more common cultural understandings ('lifeworld') have associated validity claims, seen in Table 1.

Table 1 Habermas's four main types of communicative action and their relation to forms of knowledge (Habermas 1991: 334)

Types of action	Type of knowledge embodied	Form of argumentation	Model of transmitted knowledge
Teleological action: instrumental, strategic	Technically and strategically useful knowledge	Theoretical discourse	Technological strategies
Constative speech acts (conversation)	Empirical-theoretical knowledge	Theoretical discourse	Theories
Normatively regulated action	Moral-practical knowledge	Practical discourse	Legal and moral representations
Dramaturgical action	Aesthetic practical knowledge	Therapeutic and aesthetic critique	Works of art

Ideally, political discourse is marked by a concern with moral and ethical questions which are seen in Kantian 'deontological' terms as non-arbitrary and universal in nature (even though Habermas has argued that his universalism is more delimited, sociological, than Kant's own (Calhoun et al. 1993: 64)). Habermas argues that we identify the legitimacy of these claims by innately recognizing their appeal to truthfulness. However, Habermas recognizes that political debates are often articulated with technical knowledge which may not be ethical-moral or universal in nature (or may be mixed).

The theory of communicative action is grounded in speech pragmatics from which Habermas distinguishes differences in validity claims by the way they vary in 'illocutionary force' and claims to truthfulness:

> The meaning of sentences, and the understanding of sentence meanings, cannot be separated from language's inherent relation to the validity of statements. Speakers and hearers understand the meaning of a sentence when they know under what conditions it is true. Correspondingly, they understand the meaning of a word when they know what contribution it makes to the capacity for truth of a sentence formed with its help. (Habermas 1991: 276–7)

As Table 1 indicates, Habermas's fundamental distinction is between 'language oriented to success' (theoretical and instrumental) and 'language oriented to reaching understanding' (practical-moral). Language oriented to reaching understanding depends on a shared lifeworld because this supplies the 'horizon of experience' which enables the illocutionary force of a sentence to be identified:

> Illocutionary results appear in the lifeworld to which the participants belong and which forms the background for their processes of reaching understanding. (Habermas 1991: 293)

This is the basis of the meaningfulness of arguments constituted in moral-practical discourse which contrasts to when communication is 'systematically distorted'. Thus Habermas contrasts communicative action to 'linguistically mediated strategic' action which is:

> those interactions in which at least one of the participants wants his speech acts to produce perlocutionary effects on his opposite number. (Habermas 1991: 295)

Habermas's focus on 'perlocutionary effects' – a speech act based on imperatives instituted by a power base (Habermas 1991: 310) – offers some comparability to Bourdieu's own views on the performative (see Chapter 3). Bourdieu's arguments on the performative suggest, in contrast, that we have to assess how journalists' reports on urban regeneration are deployed in specific, historically delimited conditions of 'felicity'. But Bourdieu's argument that we need journalists to engage with lay and alternative discourses (his Husserlian-based 'ethic'), has parallels with Habermas's concern with the colonizing role of teleological discourses in politics. Poupeau notes that Habermas drew on Husserl's conceptualization of the 'lifeworld', but that:

> this non-conceptualized knowledge remains within the framework of the classical view of the agent: that of the conscious agent. [...] Habermas [...] remains the prisoner of intellectualist positions incapable of accounting for the 'ontological complicity' between agent and world brought to light by Bourdieu. (Poupeau 2000: 78)

So, although Bourdieu's position suggests that journalists need to revise their characteristic modes of discourse (Marlière 2000), in our sense so that they might be able to better articulate lay opinion and thereby meet more critical standards of reflexivity – a form of professional 'second-break' – this would require major changes in the nature of the field. But if these 'habits' were instigated then journalists might be less prone to falling under the sway of, for example, neo-liberalist planning discourse. We noted in Chapter 2 that Couldry has pointed to how lay actors can be included in the media. He also argues that there is a need to allow 'local definitional battles some rein', and allow individuals to:

> have a stake in these battles through their own local attempts to define themselves, by appropriating common symbolic resources. (Couldry 2003b: 43)

Healey (1995: 267) also suggests that elitist forms of planning could be challenged by models of more open forms which attempt to promote 'interdiscursivity'. Similarly, journalistic discourse could develop reflexivity in which it attempts to activate lay opinion and the views of a wider range of social groups with different interests. In this way journalistic discourse could instantiate an awareness of the inequalities in symbolic and linguistic resources that its own practice is implicated in. In this respect, the role of journalists could then be one of not just reporting, but also representing in the idioms and character of lay discourses.

In following Bourdieu's ideas we have been critical of Habermas because, in a similar way to the system-functional linguistics that characterizes critical discourse analysis (see Chapter 3), the underlying Kantianism of his approach attributes universal status to 'rational' forms of communication. Bourdieu has argued that this 'depoliticizes' social relations by overlayering them with philosophical-ethical concerns, and power is subordinated due to the essentializing of 'relations of communication' which:

> is a simple reformulation of the Kantian principle of the universalization of moral judgement and no longer has anything in common with what is uncovered by the sociology of relations of symbolic power. (Bourdieu 2000: 66)

We know that for Bourdieu the question of the political is always 'bound up with language' in which the universal is part of a much more 'general discourse on the social world' (Bourdieu et al. 2008: 76). Bourdieu thus takes care to historicize rationality because what is counted as rational is a ground for action only insofar as it has been interrogated in light of conditions of symbolic violence:

> I have said [...] against all the forms of rationalist absolutism – of which the most enlightened representative today is undoubtedly Jürgen Habermas – that reason is historical through and through, and all we can do is work to create the historical conditions in which it can be deployed. This is what I call a realpolitik of reason. To fight for reason, for the undistorted communication that makes possible the rational exchange of arguments, etc., means fighting very consciously against all forms of violence, starting with symbolic violence. (Bourdieu et al. 2008: 222)

Bourdieu's conception of rationality, or the discursive realization of it, actually has more similarity to Iris Marion Young's 'standpoint' view, where justice is made relevant to its social context. This is why approaches to justice and the city stress that 'oppression and domination should be "primary terms for conceptualizing justice"' (Merrifield and Swyngedouw 1997: 7) or, as Crossley notes in relation to Bourdieu's arguments:

> Bourdieu advises us to seek out those social conditions which enable, encourage and constrain interlocutors to engage rationally with one another. The implication of this is that rather than devising ways of minimizing the impact of the social environment upon debating citizens, a fruitless task, we should be looking for ways best to secure such an impact. How can we constrain politicians, journalists, academics and artists in such a way that they best further their ends by way of furthering the ends of us all? And how can we ensure that all citizens have equal access to this 'regulated conflict'? These are not easy questions but they are more realistic than the Habermasian alternative. (Crossley 2004: 110)

'Historicizing' justice in relation to journalism in this way means it would have to recognize that it functions in a field which is structured by class inequality and especially so in relation to economic resources and access to the media. The ideal role of journalists in planning would be to represent, to 'facilitate' equal exchange between the forms of knowledge that characterize elite planning arguments, and lay responses. In this case, Habermas's abstract Kantian ideas of 'rational' discourse and procedural forms of justification fail to give any guidance in the face of these issues. Bourdieu's thinking on lay reflexivity, therefore, calls for us to challenge the self-satisfied abstractions of pseudo-scientific practices such as planning – and journalism:

> People accept without thinking – in politics as elsewhere – the division between the competent and the incompetent, amateurs and professionals: politicians of course, but also journalists and a wider category of intellectuals, who have a de facto monopoly on the production of political discourse, on political problems. I believe it is necessary to raise and constantly keep raising the problem of the legitimacy of the delegation and dispossession that this presupposes and brings about. (Bourdieu et al. 2008)

As we have seen, a key issue is that city press journalists work under a pervasive professional assumption that their discourses are 'precise', legitimate, truthful and unbiased. In contrast, Bourdieu prompts us to examine how the 'rationality' of reporting is relative, and situated by the social, economic and linguistic structuring of the field.

Bourdieu's position thus radically contrasts to Habermas's theory of discourse ethics whose Kantian transcendentalism orients it to discount empirical or 'partial' discourses, the discourses that characterize working-class life and culture and forms of 'practical reason'. As Poupeau has it: 'an analysis of the grounds of domination leads to an analysis of human action: practice for Bourdieu, action for Habermas' (Poupeau 2000: 73). But later commentators on Habermas like Negt and Kluge, and neo-Marxians like Lefebvre, address this issue and suggest ideas by which to deepen the analytical principle of 'grounding' universals sociologically. These writers show how lay – or more particularly working-class – experience of urban life is articulated in particular forms. Thus Negt and Kluge note that the working class's 'subaltern public sphere' that developed in trade unions and community-based media was organized on different principles from the bourgeois public sphere which Habermas used as a model for his idea of deliberation and publicness. The bourgeois public sphere's 'horizon of experience' functions principally for the middle class and rejects the language of politics coming from the less abstract, experiential or 'empirical' working-class public sphere (Negt and Kluge 1993: 28). Negt and Kluge argue that the bourgeois public sphere is marked by a preference for abstract forms of 'speech' in contrast to the 'tactility' of discourse of the proletarian public sphere (Negt and Kluge 1993: 46). Any real sense of participation in the public sphere for working-class subjects is, then, likely to be illusory or 'compensatory' (Negt and Kluge 1993: 56). In this respect Gardiner contrasts Bakhtin's dialogicism to Habermas and notes that:

> evaluative or contextualising judgements, which are rooted by and large in the circumstances of everyday life, cannot be easily separated from moral reflection. These are [...] coherent alternatives that do not jettison the promise of rational dialogue by embracing some sort of spurious postmodernist relativism yet do not subscribe to the Habermasian image of a disembodied and idealised public sphere. (Gardiner 2004: 32)

We have also noted one rare occasion when more directly reported speech/opinion appeared in the reports (in Article 2) that might demonstrate how such 'polyphony' might be put into practice. But this chapter has argued that city press reports on urban regeneration reveal a bias towards the 'primary definers' in the field, the institutions and personnel that generally make up urban growth coalitions. The fact remains that there simply are not enough 'voices' present in regeneration reporting today. The language of urban regeneration reporting is driven by a pervasive paralogistic assumption about regeneration that predisposes it to reproduce the standing relations of symbolic power in language and in the city. In Bourdieu's terms, the language of urban regeneration reporting thus reveals how journalists themselves fall foul 'of the violence that they practise'. Chapter 5 now looks at another dimension of the city press – the nature of its photojournalism.

5
The Body in the Press: Social Codes in Urban Photojournalism

Sociological analysis of photography occurs at various points in Bourdieu's work, particularly in *Photography: a Middle-brow Art* and the opening sections of *Distinction*. Bourdieu was also concerned with visual art and its importance more generally as a powerful locus of symbolic power, and in social and cultural classification (Bourdieu 1993a). Bourdieu recognized that photography in particular was a vital 'stake' in social classification struggles because of its immediacy and popularity. Bourdieu argues that it is in 'photographic production and judgements on photographic images that the principles of "popular taste" are expressed' (Bourdieu 1993a: 296). But because photography was an easily accessible 'middle-brow art', situated midway between more 'noble' and 'vulgar' practices (i.e. fine art vs. graffiti), it 'condemned its practitioners to create a substitute for the sense of cultural legitimacy which is given to the priests of all the legitimate arts' (Bourdieu 1993a: 131). In terms of the visual arts it is probably still true to say that photography takes up this ambiguous role and certainly the art market values art photography far less than fine art.

This chapter draws on the ideas developed by Bourdieu in his studies of photography in order to analyse photojournalistic images appearing in an evening newspaper's reports on urban planning and regeneration. Urban regeneration reports were discussed in Chapter 4 and these two chapters together make up a case study of the role of journalism in the political economy of our cities. City newspapers act as a key locus of symbolic power in the field of media and play a crucial role in presenting 'images' of their cities to their readerships, and to those further afield. Often press reports on the features pages of newspapers are produced with an eye to attracting inward investment rather than as presenting the realities of the city. But the daily trickle of news reports presents more reliable data upon which to focus when trying to assess the press's role in urban regeneration. As Bourdieu comments:

> Journalists play a central role, because among the producers of discourse it is they who [...] occupy a privileged position in the symbolic struggle to make things seen and believed. (Bourdieu et al. 2008: 323)

The contemporary press relies heavily upon photographic images as much as words in its reporting, and this chapter thus turns its attention to how photojournalism plays a part in the broader news process which creates 'images of the city'. From a Bourdieusian point of view we can say that photojournalistic images create and reinforce stereotypes of working-class subjects as denizens of the 'low' life of the city. We will look firstly at the distinctive nature of photojournalism in the regional press and then outline the nature of the corpus of press photographs gathered from one newspaper over six months and the class coding of the images. The final part of the chapter then reflects on Bourdieu's approach to analysing photography and the classic accounts of Barthes (1977) and Goffman (1979) in continuance of this book's engagement with alternative approaches to language and the media.

Modalities and social codes in city press photojournalism

At the outset, it is important to state that city evening press photojournalism has a distinct modality (Hodge and Kress 1988: 142) in comparison with other modes of photojournalism. It contrasts, chiefly, to the kind of serious documentary photojournalism of figures like Don McCullin which depends on an entirely distinct set of promotional practices, 'serious' criticism, publishing (in books or glossy magazines) and exhibition in galleries that sets it close to the 'internal' sector of the cultural field. A strong narrative code is also generally present in serious documentary photojournalism in its assumption that it can bear witness or 'tell a story'.

All forms of photojournalism share a baseline realism, in which the photograph is taken for granted as categorically 'testifying' to the presence of the photographer as witness at the scene (Solomon-Godeau 1991: 180). Realism is underpinned by Cartesian perspectivism (the centring of a unitary point of vision) in the technology and practices of photography, and as a visual ideology this makes it restrained in the use of montage, multidimensional or kaleidoscopic shots. Trick shots ('photogenia'), even blurring of background (Smith 1998: 30–2), are thus extremely rare in city press photojournalism (and most documentary photojournalism as well) because of the pervasiveness of realist tenets and a total belief in the veracity of the photographic image. However, whilst documentary photography may elaborate or critically engage with realism, routine city press photojournalism is usually unaware of, or content with, its realist assumptions. Documentary photography's stronger narrative impulse and creative or artistic expression generally always subordinates any captions and textual accompaniment. In contrast, the 'subordinate' aspect of its modality means its accompanying news story and caption are primary in the designation of meaning, even though the photograph may take up equal or more space than text on the page. City press photojournalism is generally therefore somewhat stilted and static, its narrative stasis revealed in its resort to usually stiffly posed figures and a type of patronizing portraiture. The subordinate modality of city press photojournalism means, also, its images tend to act mainly as a supplement to the news story, providing immediate and unambiguous images.

The accompanying figures are drawn from an analysis of photographic images contained in 132 reports on urban regeneration appearing in a UK city newspaper during the course of six months. The images used as examples in this chapter represent typical ones from 62 'portrait' images of either individuals or groups which overwhelmingly characterized the photojournalism collected in the corpus. These images were in turn classified into the following 'sets': central government figures' visits to the region (17), stock photographs of city councillors or other local key figures (16), photographs of figures from the business world (18) and community and public housing issues (11). The image of the city that comes across from this newspaper is, then, a highly 'personated' one due to the reliance by the city press on the 'genre' of portraiture.

The underlying interpretive 'ground' of these images, however, has to be seen in the broader context of developments in contemporary class issues in the politics of the city – particularly the global forces shaping cities, post-Fordism, and city centre gentrification. Bourdieu (and Champagne) in *The Weight of the World* noted in the late 1990s how the Paris press's representation of the 'problem of the suburbs' (Bourdieu 1999: 213) generally acted to reinforce negative or 'phantasmal' representations of the working class and immigrants in this political context:

> These days, referring to a 'problem suburb' or 'ghetto' almost automatically brings to mind, not 'realities' – largely unknown in any case to the people who rush to talk about them – but phantasms, which feed on emotional experiences stimulated by more or less uncontrolled words and images, such as those conveyed in the tabloids and by political propaganda or rumour. (Bourdieu 1999: 123)

But in his more direct sociological analyses of photography in *Distinction* and *Photography: a Middle-brow Art* Bourdieu also sees photography, either in popular or professional practices, as acting as an 'index and instrument of integration' of any particular social group. Photographs produced by different social groups presented a valuable source of visual data for examining how social classes distinguish and define themselves in visual terms. Similarly, city press photojournalism is also likely to be produced on the basis of the social coding of the visual field.

Just as in relation to language, Bourdieu focuses his analysis of photography at the level of 'parole' – the more obvious differences in aesthetic choices in framing and composition made by photographers:

> The taking of the picture is still a choice involving aesthetic and ethical values; if ... the nature and development of photographic technology tends to make everything 'photographable' ... it is still true that ... each group chooses a finite and well defined range of subjects, genres and compositions. (Bourdieu 1990c: 6)

In *Photography: a Middle-brow Art* Bourdieu was largely concerned with the way lay people of different classes deploy different aesthetic codes in their domestic photography. He compared middle-class and working-class camera clubs and peasants' domestic and family photography. In this work Bourdieu anticipated his criticism of the 'bourgeois aesthetic' in *Distinction* (which actually opens with discussion of the data presented in *Photography: a Middle-brow art*). Bourdieu points out how professional photographers unconsciously adopt Kantian principles of 'disinterestedness' when consciously reflecting on their practice. In contrast, working-class photographers tend to subordinate the photograph to its social function – Bourdieu giving as an example the type of 'clumsy' posing of family members in front of famous tourist sites. In contrast, professional photographers were found to:

> technically exploit the ordinary representation of photographic objectivity or on the contrary attempt to load a 'realistic' figuration with symbolic content. (Bourdieu 1990c: 101)

More recent research has also found that this conscious desire on the part of professional photographers to distance themselves from lay practices continues in the training of photographers (Newbury 1997: 429). Crucially, Bourdieu also viewed everyday photography as revealing any particular social class's 'image of its own integration' (Bourdieu 1990c: 26). But press photojournalists have to represent other class subjects and this must mean that their images are likely to reveal more general social codings, of class and status, of difference and distance (rather than identity).

In the analysis of the corpus, four main codes became apparent: the 'mise-en-scène' of the photograph – differences in location/ space; differences in clothing props and other aspects of embodiment in the 'spatial code'. Also found were consistent variations in the characteristic 'gaze' or 'look' of different class subjects. Thirdly, contrasts in the relative size/'functional ranking' of different class subjects were found to be an important 'axis' of composition in the photographs. Finally, the photographs were coded in relation to the overall status of each group in terms of their comparative 'rights to the city', something coming from the intersecting of the various codes in any one photograph. Within each of these codings two key polarities were used to describe the contrasts – for example, that between narcissistic and voyeuristic gaze codes. These findings are summarized in Table 2 and the process of interpretation and coding of the images is outlined in the next sections.

Table 2 Summary: social codings of routine urban photojournalism

Social codes	Middle-class subjects	Working-class subjects
Spatial code	Eutopic/centre (11)	Community/periphery (7)
Gaze code	Narcissistic (15/18)	Voyeuristic (7/11)
Functional ranking	High (13/18)	Low (6/11)
Status code	Proprietor/owner occupier (18)	Client/tenant (8)

Note: Numbers in brackets indicate occurrences in divisions between middle-class and working-class subjects in the portrait images' 'set' as a whole.

Spatial and status code

The key topic of urban regeneration reporting and its accompanying photojournalism is, of course, the city and spatial issues. Similarly, in the process of depicting different subjects their class is generally encoded by the situation or locale they are most often identified with. Thus, in his long-standing concern with embodiment and language Bourdieu (with Merleau-Ponty in mind) notes this coding of space and the body in representations of urban life:

> As bodies (and biological individuals), and in the same way that things are, human beings are situated in a site (they are not endowed with the ubiquity that would allow them to be in several places at once), and they occupy a place. The *site* (*le lieu*) can be defined absolutely as the point in *physical space* where an agent or thing is situated, 'takes place', exists: that is to say, either as a *localization* or, from a relational viewpoint, as a *position*, a rank in an order. The place occupied may be defined as the extent, surface and volume that an individual or a thing occupies in physical space, its dimensions, or better still, its 'bulk' (as is sometimes said of a vehicle or piece of furniture). (Bourdieu 1999: 123–4)

City press photojournalism draws on this type of social coding of the body, space and demeanour in its compositional practices because photojournalists intuitively work through common understandings about the social world. Because the subjects of photography unconsciously display their class identity via body demeanour, Bourdieu is thus pointing to how everyday social-codifications of our sense of self and others, referred to by Walter Benjamin as 'body and image space (*Lieb- und Bildrain*)' (Weigel 1996: x), can be seen in photographic and other forms of visual representation.

Differences in bodily demeanour (hexis) are, then, assumed by subjects in acts of self-classification. But other acts of social classification are the result of the compositional decisions of photojournalists who also intuitively deploy social codes in their representational practices, seeing people in relation to their 'canonic generality' (Burgin 1997: 82). Spatial codes thus prompt photojournalists to classify and stereotype working-class subjects as a result of these broader ideologies of the particular urban 'locales' in which that class is associated. Lefebvre argued that the image of the city has a 'paradigmatic' aspect which impacts on discursive practices more generally – particularly in the contrast between public and private home ownership:

> [The city] has a *paradigmatical* dimension; it implies and shows oppositions, the inside and outside, the centre and the periphery, the integrated and non-integrated to urban society. […] If we consider the sector of owner-occupation and that of new social housing estates, we already know that each of them constitutes a (partial) system of significations, and that another system which over-determines each of them is established from their opposition. (Lefebvre et al. 1996: 116)

The social-spatial contrast between the centre of cities (once the locus of 'inner-city' problems but since the 1990s and gentrification now the site of new middle-class habitués) and periphery/estates is a key code in the city press. This coding can be seen at work in Figures 5 and 6. There is an obvious contrast in the two images in the way differences in clothing identify the subjects' class. Working-class subjects usually appear in problem (crime, urban decay) stories, whilst middle-class subjects are predominantly positively depicted in reports on success. Middle-class subjects are also usually depicted as smiling whilst the facial expressions of working-class subjects are usually more serious. There is also a contrast here between stereotypical spatial props of working-class city life, fences, waste bins, in Figure 6 and the slick city centre environment of the middle-class subject in Figure 5.

The social coding of urban space thus acts as a key discursive structure in city press photojournalism. The corpus reveals many

Figure 5 'Destination: Manchester' (*Manchester Evening News*, 12 August 2009, p. 9, Features)

more of the middle-class subjects to be associated with the 'centre' of the city – business and management – whilst working-class subjects were nearly always depicted in the 'periphery', the zones of manual labour and the service industries. This spatial distinction instils a sense of differences in citizen status between the middle class as citizens and the working class as outsiders or 'denizens'. This visual-form of subordination in photojournalism is also part of the *realpolitiks* of contemporary urban regeneration in our cities – the process of middle-class 'usurpation' of the city centre. Figures 5 and 6 also show how historically, working-class people have been associated more with the 'enclave of "community" and mutual dependence' (McDowell 2000: 399) whilst the gentrifying middle class, in contrast, is now associated with the 'eutopic' space (Davis 2006: 6) of the postmodernizing city. Eutopic space and post-Fordism are now the dominant urban aesthetic of the 'main street' (Graham 1997: 120), associated with international business and tourism, lying between airports and other new communications networks such as

Figure 6   'Don't bulldoze homes, say families on hit list' (*Manchester Evening News*, 22 July 2009, p. 19, News)

'technopoles' (Castells and Hall 1994). The contrast between these two photographs is a materialization of the culture of postmodernism and the service economy, the larger political-economic context of city photojournalism.

Functional ranking

So, in deciphering the spatial codes of city press photojournalism we have to look to structures lying beyond the actual photo in order to interpret them. In the quote above Bourdieu refers to the relative 'bulk' of space any individual might inhabit. Similarly, the idea of 'functional ranking' is used by Goffman in *Gender Advertisements* to indicate how implicit understandings of the gender hierarchy in which men dominate enter much more broadly into the framing of photographic subjects in the world of PR and advertising. Functional ranking is an aspect of the way professional photographers have to compose their images in order to overcome the problem of the 'camera's straight on eye' (Goffman 1979: 18). Functional ranking is thus assessed by taking stock of how photographers:

> Position the characters in the picture microecologically so that their placement relative to one another will provide an index of mapping their presumed social position relative to one another. (Goffman 1979: 26)

But we can also think of social ranking in terms 'not simply of distance, but also of categories of people' (Hodge and Kress 1988: 55). Functional ranking has this type of role in city press photojournalism as exemplified by Figures 5 and 7. Here middle-class subjects smile confidently and peer down onto the camera. In contrast, the photographs of working-class men in Figures 6 and 8 place them in a much lower functional ranking and they do not dominate the field of vision to the same extent. In this manner, functional ranking in photojournalism acts to reinforce the coding of status and space in the treatment of different class subjects. Functional ranking is the result of the process of the photojournalist prompting, cueing and posing subjects on an intuitive understanding of class and other differences in social esteem. This will also probably play a part in editorial choices between any number of alternative images that may have resulted from the original 'shoot'.

But representing people is always a two-way process, as Bourdieu notes in relation to his study of the French Béarn peasants' experience of the professional photographer's 'gaze':

> Thus it is understandable that the taking of photographs always provokes a certain unease, especially among peasants, who are most often condemned to internalise the pejorative image that the members of other groups have of them, and who therefore have a poor relationship to their own bodies. (Bourdieu 1990c: 83)

Similarly, Spence's work on photography notes that 'in our society most of the "messages" received by the working class are mediated via the middle class' (Spence 1995: 39) either by journalists more

4 » BUSINESS PROFESSIONALS

Grant Thornton boss starts own consultancy

■ Whittaker will still work with GT in future

■ Grundy is one of youngest office heads

KEVIN FEDDY

GRAEME Whittaker, managing partner of accountancy firm **Grant Thornton's** Manchester office, is leaving to set up his own business and will be replaced by David Grundy, it was announced today.

Mr Grundy, 41, who joined GT as a graduate trainee, will become one of the firm's youngest-ever managing partners when he takes over at the helm of the Spinningfields office, which has 350 staff.

The married father of two has worked in various senior role across the business, most recently as UK head of transactional services.

Mr Whittaker, who is leaving

after 25 years, joined GT in Manchester in 1984 and was office managing partner between 1993 and 2007.

He then spent a year in London launching the firm's national entrepreneurial advisory operations before returning to his old role at the end of 2008, when he succeeded John Shinnick.

Now Mr Whittaker is leaving to establish a consultancy to identify equity opportunities and help with companies' restructuring and reorganisation plans. He will continue to work closely with GT in his new venture. "Although I am leaving to develop other opportunities, we will be working together on projects. I wish David every success with the new role," said Mr Whittaker.

Mr Grundy said he was 'relishing' the challenges ahead.

"It's a tough market but we have a fantastic team and every confidence in the region's ability to lead the way out of the downturn," he said.

"Manchester does have a base of talent and entrepreneu-

» **FROM TRAINEE TO MANAGING PARTNER** David Grundy is taking over after the departure of Graeme Whittaker

rial spirit that you simply don't find elsewhere.

"The advent of Media City and the quality of region's transport infrastructure, in particu-

lar the airport, will help the city grow further still and confirm its reputation as one of Europe's most attractive provincial capitals."

Figure 7 'Grant Thornton boss starts own consultancy' (*Manchester Evening News*, 30 July 2009, p. 4, Business)

generally, or by professional photographers. Different degrees of 'stress' conditioned in part by the relative status differentials between photographer and subject might explain, be a factor in, the contrast between the relaxed bodily demeanour of the two middle-class men in Figures 5 and 7 and the stiltedness in working-class men in Figures 6 and (to a lesser extent) 8.

Gaze

The conjuncture of codes of spatial location and functional ranking together is part of the process in the production of city press photojournalistic images. These images start to make their subjects act as 'metonyms' of status in relation to larger class identities. Additionally, the corpus also exhibited consistent differences in expression between

M.E.N. MONDAY JULY 6, 2009

£300,000 fillip for Church St market

- Council revamp will double stall numbers

- Customers 'have been coming for decades'

| BEN ROOTH

MANCHESTER city centre market will double in size as a result of a £300,000 investment by Manchester city council.

The Church Street outdoor market – which is across the High Street from the Arndale

Market – currently consists of five stalls selling books, fruit and vegetables, clothes, hats and records.

The stalls will be demolished in January and replaced with 11 new ones made from steel, glass and shutters, decorated with street art murals.

The development is intended to create an additional attraction in the city centre.

Mark Legunski, head of Manchester Markets, said: "We have all the finance in place and planning permission agreed, so we plan to start work on demolishing the old stalls, which have become rather tired, and start rebuilding the

new look market towards the end of January next year.

"The existing stallholders have been offered stalls and we already have traders lined up for the additional six stalls, which will include a food outlet."

Coun Pat Karney, Manchester city council's spokesman on the city centre, added: "This is an exciting project that will provide an attraction for shoppers to cross High Street from the Arndale market and draw them towards other businesses

in the Northern Quarter of the city centre."

Fruit and vegetable vendor Mark McCall, who has run his stall in central Manchester for 30 years, said that it was the 'dawn of a new era'.

He said: "There's incredible affection for this market, and many of our customers have been coming here for decades.

"It's undoubtedly the dawn of a new era, and I hope that the venue never loses any of the individuality which makes it so popular."

Bookseller Eddie Hopkinson, who has operated a stall in central Manchester for 40 years, said: "The investment in this market is very much to be welcomed.

"There is slight concern among stallholders about the short length of the three-year leases we are all being offered – particularly as it's going to cost each of us thousands to kit out new stall out.

"But this will hopefully be resolved in the fullness of time."

>> NEW ERA Stallholders Mark McCall, left, and Eddie Hopkinson outside their units in Church Street market in Manchester: they welcomed the council's initiative

Figure 8 '£300,000 fillip for Church St market' (*Manchester Evening News*, 6 July 2009, p. 23, Business)

middle-class and working-class subjects. This was coded in relation to the concept of 'gaze' or 'look', common elements recognized as characterizing in the 'microecology' of portrait photographs. The gaze is also seen as contributing to the 'evidential force' of the rhetoric of the photographic image (Hirsch 1997: 6). Walker and Chaplin identify at least three key 'looks' occurring in photographs of people: that of the 'artist' (or photographer), the exchange of looks which may be taking place within the image, and the look of the 'eye' or spectator (Walker and Chaplin 1997: 97–9). Solomon-Godeau notes two key gazes – 'narcissistic' and 'voyeuristic' (Solomon-Godeau 1991: 197). A 'narcissistic gaze' is confident, self-assured and returns the viewers' gaze whist a 'voyeuristic' gaze is insecure, averted. The selected figures show how narcissistic gazes characterized the photographs of middle-class subjects and this compositional aspect served to reinforce the generally more positive framings and functional ranking of them. In contrast, a voyeurist gaze was more regularly found in photographs of working-class subjects.

Bourdieu and the analysis of the photographic image

The above analysis of press photography has followed the general principles of Bourdieu's approach to photography and been, essentially,
pitched at the level of 'parole', the codes revealed 'in' the images. But
we have to see how the relations 'within' and between the photographs
need to be contextualized by the social and political field – forces like
post-Fordism. This contrasts to structuralist analysis of the image,
in relation to the principles of analysis of language more generally
(discussed in Chapter 1) where the meaning of single images or words
has to be found in relation to larger discourses or context. The classic
structuralist analysis of the photographic image is Barthes's (1977), and
being heavily influenced by Saussurian linguistics he argued that it is
only possible to read the social coding of the photographic image at its
'secondary level' of connotation or rhetorical practices (camera work,
positioning). This might at first sight seem to agree with Bourdieu – that
social analysis of the photographic image lies at the level of parole. But
Barthes's analysis contrasts to Bourdieu's because of the 'analogonic'
nature of the process of production of the photographic image. In this
view, the analogic camera technology of the pre-digital era provided
a highly denotative form of representation which essentially means
that no ideologically informed act imposes itself between the signified
and signifiers (Barthes 1977: 44). In this sense, Barthes argues that the
photograph carries a 'message without a code'.

This view has influenced key analysts of photography during the
'high tide' of structuralism, such as Burgin, who argued that it is more
useful to explore universal orientations in perception as they become
revealed in individual photographs (Burgin 1982: 70). Burgin hoped,
long before digital camera technology became established, that
the electronic-digital 'banking' of images would facilitate just such
a Barthean conventional structuralist analysis of the photograph
(Burgin 1982: 62–3). Barthes himself looked to establish the codes of
the language of images in terms of intertextuality, how the photograph is part of a 'complex of concurrent messages' (Barthes 1981).
Similarly, Sekula argued that the photograph is an 'incomplete utterance, a message that depends on some external matrix of conditions
and presuppositions for its readability' (Sekula 1981: 453).

As a result of this kind of inherent formalism, structuralist analysis
of the photographic image has had a type of 'temerity in the face of the

social' which does not figure in Bourdieu's analysis. Bourdieu's analysis suggests subjects act to translate the social coding of the visual field into photographic (and other) practices. But the structuralists' concern with the denotative quality of the photograph means that they reject seeing a single image as a complete 'utterance'. However, just as Bourdieu countered structuralist anthropological arguments in *The Logic of Practice* and in *Language and Symbolic Power* in relation to language, in the case of the photographic image he also counters such arguments by pointing to the social processes involved in the constitution of the photograph.

Bourdieu's approach thus accords with the more technical arguments made against structuralism by Lefebvre who points out:

> When codes worked up from literary texts are applied to spaces – to urban spaces, say – we remain, as may easily be shown, on the purely descriptive level. Any attempt to use such codes as a means of deciphering social space must surely reduce that space itself to the status of a *message*, and the inhabiting of it to the status of a *reading*. This is to evade both history and practice. (Lefebvre 1991: 7)

In contrast, this chapter has argued that Bourdieu makes us point to the intuitive 'choices' ('of the necessary') made by press photographers as being influenced by the social coding of the visual field. Because city life is central to urban photojournalism, the social coding of space plays a crucial role in the practice. Bourdieu's arguments in relation to the stereotyping of the suburbs, the press's visual (and verbal) depictions of the urban, and his studies of habituated nature of photographic practice shows the multidimensional nature in the conditioning of these images, and their instantiation in the politics of the city and citizenship.

Although this chapter has drawn on Goffman's seminal analysis of the role of functional ranking in photography, there are many contrasts with Bourdieu's own approach. I have argued that consistent differences occur in the social coding of city press photography. In contrast, Goffman relied on easy-to-hand data of print advertisements from a number of publications and his selection was somewhat idiosyncratic, and therefore not easy to make comparative study. In contrast, the above analysis and the underlining of the class codings in urban photojournalism of *one* newspaper invites comparative study.

Goffman nevertheless felt confident that the corpus he collected could be used to indicate '"small behaviours" where physical forms are well codified' (Goffman 1979: 24–5). Goffman realized that it was not really possible in analysing photographs to be sure about how gender actually *is* performed. Nevertheless he felt it was possible to say something about their naturalness as *photographic* representations. But Goffman actually made little attempt to move beyond this type of 'anthropology' of 'gender displays' (Goffman 1979: 3). In contrast, Bourdieu shows us how larger social forces, the forces that shape the body and social space, are present in routine urban photojournalism. Similarly, in her study of documentary photography Solomon-Godeau notes that we must ask:

> whether the documentary act does not involve a double act of subjugation: first, in the social world that has produced its victims; and second, in the regime of image produced within and for the same system that engenders the conditions that it then re-presents. (Solomon-Godeau 1991: 176)

In Chapter 1 we noted that the key factor in the analysis of language for Bourdieu was whether the issue focused on, such as talk radio, plays a role in symbolic violence. This principle makes the features examined 'sociologically significant' rather than, as in structuralist analyses, formally significant. The social coding of the visual field we have seen in routine urban photojournalism has, if we agree with Solomon-Godeau, very real repercussions for our everyday understanding of urban life and how we perceive the citizenship status of different classes. City press photojournalism plays a significant part, therefore, in the broader process of symbolic violence associated with post-Fordism and city centre gentrification. Castells famously noted that the material displacement of the working classes from the centre of European cities in the 1960s had the effect of splitting their political consciousness (Castells and Lebas 1978: 27–9). By following Bourdieu we have been able to see how the social coding of routine urban photojournalism, similarly, serves to divide, envision and act to differentiate the working class's and middle class's 'rights to the city'.

6
Voice, Radio, Field

Voice and the media

This chapter uses interview and other original data drawn from research into how language might figure as an issue in the field of local radio in the Greater Manchester area. Unstructured interviews were held with representative figures on this topic, drawn from across the range of radio broadcasting in the Manchester area, using the idea of field-positional sampling. Like most local and regional fields of the media, the Manchester area yielded up representative institutions running across community, public service radio and commercial stations, as well as local offices of state regulators (in the UK this is OFCOM). This approach produced interviews of approximately one hour's length with sixteen key figures involved in radio broadcasting in the area. As a result of this research the case of a community radio station, Caribbean Carnival Radio, presented a number of key issues in relation to the themes of this book.

As introduced in Chapter 3, the concept of voice can be used to develop Bourdieu's account of language in order to take account of lay-reflexivity in language in general, and in relation to media practices like radio. However, voice has been used in quite a number of ways within culture and communications studies, including studies of oral culture, narratology in literary studies, and in media studies of various forms of representational practices (Atkinson 1999). However, in these studies, voice tends to be synonymous with literary concepts such as style, narrative, culture, representation or life history, and its specificity as a concept relating to spoken discourse is often obscured.

This chapter aims to demonstrate how Bourdieu's theory of symbolic violence in language can be elaborated in such a way as to include consideration of 'field effects' – the state of relations of symbolic power as a structural force – but also as able to account for instances of symbolic struggle 'from below'. In this sense, then, we turn from the more 'internalist' or textual focus of Chapters 4 and 5, to how music figures in radio as an aspect of 'voice', and in turn how both music and voice need to be understood relationally – in reference to the field's structure of differences.

One of the problems of articulating the concept of voice within a sociological and critical approach to language and the media, however, is that it has connotations of essentialism. For instance, in Heidegger's view of speech, voice is seen as the articulation of a group's self-identify – its social being:

> To speech belong the speakers, but not as cause to effect. Rather in speech the speakers have their presencing. Where to? Presencing to the wherewithal of their speech, to that by which they linger, that which in any given situation already matters to them. Which is to say, their fellow human beings and the things, each in its own way; everything that makes a thing a thing and everything that sets the tone for our relations with our fellows. (Heidegger 1993: 406–7)

But we need to stipulate at the outset that voice is also socially evaluated, and this means it also indicates the status or prestige of different accents and dialects within a common language (Hudson 1980: 38). Seen in this way, variations in voice do not mean that it simply expresses variations in the experience and identities of different social groups. Bourdieu's approach stimulates us into thinking of voice in relational terms, as something that is produced in symbolic struggle. Bourdieu states that the linguistic aspects of the habitus act to condition our actions in the cognitive, as well as embodied, senses:

> Language does not reduce, as we often think, to a more or less extensive collection of words. As syntax it provides us with a system of transposable mental dispositions. These go hand in hand with roles which dominate the whole of our experience and, in particular, with a vision of society and culture. (Bourdieu et al. 1994: 8)

But voice seems to be something that arises from the interaction of individuals united in creating sense, creating messages, in music, radio as well as speech or written expression. Voice can thus also help to identify how experience inscribed in the habitus of any particular social group is articulated in and against the 'standing relations' of symbolic power lying in the field. Voice allows us to maintain a grasp on how the experiential, the intuitive side of the linguistic habitus finds particular forms of expression due to the nature of this or that field – to find a place within it that is not immediately 'automatic' and available in the structure of relations set there, but might be in some way 'created'. It is in this sense that we can see the field of local radio as offering an 'arena of voice' in the context of the larger media field.

Thinking more specifically about music radio means we have to see voice in relation, also, to what Barthes refers to as a place which deals in the 'grain of voice'. Barthes discusses voice in relation to music by noting that the 'geno-song' acts in music in a similar way to the 'implicatures' (Scannell 1991: 6) of voice in speech – surpassing the basic communicative function of any message. But we know that just what music gets played on music radio depends on conditions in the field and whether opportunity – air time – is acquired. Once a particular form of music is accepted in the mainstream media, it can then serve to enhance the symbolic power of the generation associated with it. For example, in Albert-Honore's study of black American radio it is noted that when black Americans gained editorial control of their own stations in the late 1940s they 'achieved voice', and this was vital because 'history belongs to those who can speak for themselves' (Albert-Honore 1992: 3).

The situation of black radio in the UK is not that dissimilar to the situation Albert-Honore notes in relation to America in the 1940s. There are still very few opportunities, particularly due to state licensing and commercial restrictions, for Afro-Caribbeans (for example) to gain voice in the field of radio. Yet Caribbean dialect or patois is both a culturally significant 'grain of voice' (in reggae, rap, calypso) and an important everyday speech dialect in the UK. David Sutcliffe's extensive study of British Black English has noted the important role of patois in marking the language because 'although close to the white norm ... [it] remains distinctively black' (Sutcliffe 1984: 219). The distinctiveness of British Black English marks it off from Jamaican Creole (which its speakers often switch to) and this suggests that the two dialects have distinct functions for each community. A Black English dialect may also be marked by highly localized areal identifications, in the way that Bajan rather than Jamaican Creole is the principal West Indian dialect in Reading (Sutcliffe 1984). Thus, even though the primary function of any dialect is as a distinguisher of cultural and other differences in the larger language community (Hudson 1980: 34), dialect also acts as a vital marker of voice. However, just as regional accents or dialects are subordinate to RP and standard English, Afro-Caribbean accents are also subordinated, as seen in the following quote:

> One of the advantages of using Standard English is its range of styles, from the most colloquial (and slangy) to the most stiffly formal. This passage [i.e. Jamaican Creole] exposes the apparently very limited stylistic register of this dialect. (Honey 1997: 39–40)

By tracing one line of the manifestation of Caribbean voice in the context of the field of British radio we can counter the self-satisfied nature of this type of argument and begin to understand the arbitrary nature of pronouncements based upon the institutionalization of Standard English and RP.

Introductory points: voice and Caribbean Carnival Radio

This section argues that by broadcasting in a marked Afro-Caribbean dialect Caribbean Carnival Radio was able to articulate a particular, identifiable, voice in its music and spoken word. The voice that this community radio station articulated was perceived by its inner-city black audience as more relevant to its life and culture than mainstream radio broadcasting by the BBC and commercial stations. In articulating the cultural experience and values of its own community and distinct inner-city urban location, Caribbean Carnival Radio shows how voice is an aspect of lay-reflexivity in language in the media field.

Although able to call on the technical expertise of Afro-Caribbean entrepreneurs in Manchester's music industry Carnival Radio's programming was community-directed and, more importantly, community 'voiced'. In this way it was able to articulate 'structures of relevance' (Hollander and Stoppers 1992: 21). The Afro-Caribbean community that the station served has a high percentage of private landlord or council-provided housing and has gained widespread national notoriety as an area associated with violence and drugs. Manchester's Afro-Caribbean community started to locate to the area during the 1960s when property values were fairly low due to the deteriorating condition of the Victorian and Edwardian housing in the area, and the out-movement of white working-class people to new council estates outside the inner-city. A number of notoriously bad public housing schemes in the 1970s contributed to the poor image of the area which was compounded by high local unemployment rates. In 1981 the area became a site of riots during the widespread public disturbances and unrest in England during the summer of that year. However, during the mid-1990s a significant improvement in the urban environment occurred as a result of government initiatives and public–private regeneration partnerships. Today, although still facing many difficulties, the Afro-Caribbean community is well into its second generation and remains the distinctive one in the area, but still has to counter negative stereotypes in the mainstream media and elsewhere.

The first point to make here is that Carnival Radio wanted to appeal to its audience in terms of 'diasporic' cultural identity, a paradoxical but nevertheless distinctive, 'knowable' community. A key feature for such success in a community radio station is, as Drijvers puts it, a 'clear insight into the social stratification of the communities they are attempting to serve' (Drijvers 1992: 199). Carnival Radio understood this because it realized that its biggest asset lay in its knowledge of the distinct cultural concerns of its community:

> [We had] an image of radio and of community. We know the community and from an entertainment's point of view I know the community and there is a certain image [of that] just as there are certain people who listen to Radio One [the BBC's national pop music station]. (Carnival Radio)

And this meant knowing, also, how it was *different* from other stations, either in areal terms, in terms of cultural rather than economic driving forces, as well as in socio-economic terms. Whilst concerned with 'authenticity' – projecting a voice that was distinctive and reverberative of the local community and Caribbean culture – it nevertheless took up a critical position when seen in the context of the entire field of local radio.

The station's principal aim in creating a musical voice was to broadcast 'soca-calypso' music – a West Indian, fairly recent, development in song which melds soul and reggae. But Caribbean Carnival Radio had to placate the state regulators of radio – OFCOM – who stipulate that all stations have to provide a varied range of programming. The station therefore also had to include regular local news slots and feature programmes alongside soca-calypso:

> [W]e were trying to establish a Caribbean type radio station which was not just soul or reggae-based but a Caribbean station with lots of information about things that are happening. The sort of thing that at one o'clock in the afternoon you can hear about things Caribbean, a Caribbean recipe or whatever. It wasn't just the music it was the information side of things as well. [...] [I]f there was a template it was [our experience in] ICR [Independent Community Radio] but that didn't include features, or a lot of the soca and calypso. The thing with carnival week is that a lot of people, black white or whatever want to learn a lot about Caribbean lifestyle and the plan was to keep the radio station going on so that people could learn about it all the time. (Carnival Radio)

The station clearly wanted to produce broadly educative but also entertaining programming. This was felt as resonating with the complex cultural and social needs of its Afro-Caribbean community which was seen in dual-spatial terms as particular to the *inner-city* yet having West Indian 'roots'. So the desire to be local was tempered by the need to transmit a voice resonant of contemporary Caribbean popular culture. Thus one of the station's key linking phrases was 'the sounds you would hear at one o'clock in the afternoon in Trinidad':

> The great thing for me when people were talking about the radio station was everyone kept saying 'Caribbean station what does it mean?' One phrase we used was 'at one o'clock in the afternoon you can hear a soul song followed by a calypso type song, which is Caribbean soul, which you can hear at one o'clock in the afternoon if you were in Trinidad or somewhere in the Caribbean'. So that was what we were doing because there are people in this country who have lived there and that is what they listen to anyway. So we would get that audience and so have that continuity. (Carnival Radio)

As Hall notes, this concern is one that stimulates local roots against the forms of symbolic violence that are associated with global corporate and media power:

> It is a respect for local roots which is brought to bear against the anonymous, impersonal world of the globalized forces which we do not understand. 'I can't speak of the world but I can speak of my neighbourhood, I can speak of my community'. The face-to-face communities that are knowable, that are locatable, one can give them a place. One knows what the voices are. (Hall 1991: 35)

And, as Hall goes on to note, a reforging of the relationship between voice, accent, dialect and place is increasingly important as a means to create symbolic counter-strategies to homogenizing discourses in global society:

> Modern theories of enunciation always oblige us to recognize that enunciation comes from somewhere. It cannot be unplaced, it cannot be unpositioned, it is always positioned in a discourse. It is when a discourse forgets that it is placed that it tries to speak to everybody else. (Hall 1991: 36)

The following quote contrasts how this 'localized' form of voice was produced with just such an awareness of the failure of earlier attempts by commercial community radio stations:

> We said to them what you have got planned isn't going to work because you are saying you are an inner-city radio station but you have pretensions of trying to capture a more inclusive audience and there is a very specific audience inside the inner cities which you should aim at and once you show the people of the inner-city that this is for them you will get their support. (Carnival Radio)

In contrast, Caribbean Carnival Radio was immediately perceived by its local audience as both relevant and popular:

> The main aspect of the station was that people warmed to it and when it went off we had people coming up to us and saying 'when are you coming back on?' Even some of the presenters and DJs

who had been on pirate stations were saying 'when are you coming back on?' (Carnival Radio)

The impact of the state and market: adopting a mask of 'mundanity'

One of Bourdieu's abiding concerns in relation to the field approach is to make sure any field under study is situated in relation to the 'power' fields of state and market. In Chapter 1 it was noted that the appearance of relatively new social forces, like cultural intermediaries, are often associated with shifts in relations in the linguistic field. In the UK state cultural institutions and regulators, such as OFCOM, monitor all media production including radio. So, alongside the market, the state sets some of the key parameters of symbolic power. The state's role in radio is so large in the UK that it has been seen as the final arbiter of the principal 'modes of reality' in the field and even the content of radio programmes is, in the 'final instance', governed by its logic (Hall 1972: 91). For example, BBC radio broadcasting approaches 65 per cent of all adult listeners in the UK (BBC Annual Report 2005–6).

Carnival Radio operated on a 28-day Restricted Service Licence (RSL), a licence that is granted by OFCOM mainly to accompany cultural events or festivals of various kinds generally in urban areas. Four hundred and thirty-two short-term RSLs were licensed in 2007 and most of these (two-thirds) went to special events. But any group applying for a licence has to demonstrate to the regulator considerable levels of technical expertise and a clear business plan. Caribbean Carnival Radio met the technical requirements of setting up and using broadcasting equipment and studio facilities because it was able to draw on the quite extensive experience amongst its organizers in pirate and mainstream radio and music industry DJ work.

The overarching role of OFCOM means that it acts not only to ensure technical requirements are met, but also to monitor professional and cultural standards. The predecessor of OFCOM, the Radio Authority, was seen as an essentially 'right wing' (Gray and Lewis 1992: 163) cultural authority and when it was established in the mid-1990s the British state started to look at radio as a dual system of commercial Independent Local Radio stations on seven-year licences, alongside BBC local radio. The Radio Authority claimed that there was a shortage of radio frequencies, but Lewis and Booth argue that this is a 'myth' used by the state to justify its paternalism and close control of the medium (Lewis and Booth 1989: xviii).

The duopoly in the structure of British radio of public service broadcasting and commercial stations thus works to exclude a huge but heterogeneous and socially differentiated audience which could be exploited by smaller stations able to access the 'structures of relevance' of more distinct communities. The paternalist constraint of radio by the British state means that the market for a greater range of stations and cultural expression is unnecessarily restricted. Although today OFCOM is supposed to ensure that radio provision reflects the full range of communities in the country, and all stations pay lip service to this need in one way or another when making their applications for licences, in practice this is soon forgotten. Commercial stations actually argue that their preference for social anonymity is a result of the nature of the licensing agreements the stations have to make with OFCOM:

> Our licence was granted on the basis that we will deliver a particular type of music. It's nothing to do with social democracy – it's all to do with choice. The BBC has a bigger obligation to do that. Our obligation is to cover audiences. So we tend to put most of our time and money into researching what most people want to listen to. So that is really what we deliver, so it doesn't matter where you live.
> (Commercial Radio Station, Manchester)

In the process of competition for local area licences, all stations tend to claim they will serve the particular communities within their transmission area. But, due to competing pressures, commercial stations 'quickly shed their mantle of localism, as they form networks for ad sales and cross ownership with newspapers and TV stations' (Dunaway 1998: 93). The organizers of Carnival Radio were very aware of these problems:

> Even when we come down to the [commercial] music stations like Kiss FM, when they put their submissions in they were different, listen to them now and they are all identical. But they said they would have reggae, ethnic music, that is how they got their licences, they said they would give a spread of material. Now, in

> six months or two years they are all exactly the same. They say it is
> what people want but it's what people get really. (Carnival Radio)

This homogenizing as a result of market forces is compounded by
the way OFCOM zealously tracks down pirate radio stations. OFCOM
states that it 'is required to satisfy itself that licensees are "fit and
proper persons"' before it grants licences and anyone convicted of
pirate broadcasting was rejected out of hand – ironic because many
DJs learn the technical and presentational aspects of radio in pirate
stations.

However, due to the tight control of the radio field, Caribbean
Carnival Radio could not adopt a radically alternative style of programming and instead adapted its voice by mimicking the programming of mainstream popular music radio:

> Because it was a local station a lot of people listen to pirate sta-
> tions which as you know can be raided. But we were making
> music and features so a lot of people knew it wasn't going to be
> shut down tomorrow, so they were listening to the music, the fea-
> tures and competitions and it was good to say 'here's the address
> or phone number ...' I had to make sure we had that because if it
> was a local thing it would [otherwise] appear like a pirate station.
> (Carnival Radio)

A concern with 'being local' and being alternative whilst assuming
the mantle of normativity underlies this strategy. Also indicated in
this quote is the multilayered nature of the meanings of community,
locality and audience in the station's thinking about its voice. Voice
can be seen here in relation to Bourdieu's concern to locate the import
of any form of 'speech' in relation to the market – voice is not simply
an expression of experience, but also a relational form of language
practice.

Voice was thus able resolve a number of contradictory aims and
competing constraints facing the station. In order to negotiate the
regulatory pressures arising from state and competitive pressures from
the commercial sector the organizers needed to mimic mainstream
radio discourse, adopting a fairly competitively informed, broad-
based type of music programming (as one of its catchphrases suggests:
'Carnival 87FM, your positive community broadcaster and I mean

*broad*caster'). As the following quote shows, this concern was also driven by a need to compete with mainstream stations in the city:

> One of the other things we decided on was if we were going to play a lot of soul in the day it would be soul as in the national charts – so we are keeping that audience. And the reggae would be commercial reggae that is in the charts, and doing a lot on the dance floors and stuff like that. [...] We made sure it was commercial and getting the DJs sorted out so they were playing things that were commercial to keep the listeners. (Carnival Radio)

Nevertheless, the adoption of a voice mimicking the authoritativeness of mainstream channels also allowed the station's key concern to broadcast Caribbean music and culture and break into the local radio field in a way that was quietly subversive of its dominant order. The multilayered nature of the station's voice, therefore, resulted from an awareness of its locality, the range of social and cultural needs of its audience, and engaging with the power of mainstream radio and the state.

The grain of voice: soca-calypso

> 'Authentic, Afro-centric transmissions live from the Moss Side and Hulme Business Centre.' (Carnival Radio DJ link)

Wall has noted that studies of radio in sociology and cultural studies tend to overlook the dominant cultural form that is actually broadcast there – popular music (Wall 1998). In regard to soca-calypso the musicological literature is quite limited. Dudley's ethnomusicological study of the genre notes that soca-calypso is a relatively recent popular cultural form in the West Indies, originating in the 1970s in order to compete with commercially successful US dance music. It was thus a response to the competitive pressures of a global marketplace on music production:

> Soca reinforced the status and economic survival of the agents involved in the creation of calypso at a time when national and international economic competition was keen, by appealing to a wider audience both nationally and internationally. (Dudley 1996: 293)

In terms of its distinctive musical characteristics, Dudley notes that soca uses a much wider range of percussion instruments than calypso and has a more intense bass which is referred to as 'kick-drum pattern' (Dudley 1996: 293). Soca's genealogy is also complex because, although arising in the 1970s as a commercial response to dance, its bass has a more intense 'syncopated line' (Dudley 1996: 297) than calypso. These features also add meaning to soca's hybridity because of its mix of Latin American and Caribbean musical traditions, and its drawing on the strong Muslim East Indian tassa drum tradition in Trinidad. Dudley notes there has been a certain degree of levelling down of these musical elements due to its commercial impetus, and soca-calypso tends to have a more 'hi-tech sound with easily accessible party/dance lyrics' (Dudley 1996: 285).

Soca-calypso is, therefore, a hybrid genre made up of West Indian traditional calypso and soul and dance music – hence soca (soul and calypso). Hill, in one of the few musicological studies of calypso underlines the fact that there is actually very little that is 'traditional' in the calypso music which preceded soca. Calypso arose in the 1890s in Trinidad but its roots are hybrid, drawing on many musical genres including Venezuelan string bands, bongos and Creole carnival:

> Calypso developed in late 19th century Port of Spain, when former slaves mingled with other Creoles and once-indentured Africans in an emerging urban carnival. (Hill 1993: 22)

But there was also a radical edge or heritage to this music because, during the Caribbean's prolonged struggle for independence from Britain, calypso poets/singers were feared by the colonialists due to the political influence of its lyrics which were fashioned in response to issues of the time (Denselow 1989: 124).

However, although very popular in Trinidad (its country of origin) and the West Indies, soca-calypso is still quite rare in Britain. Because of this it has, despite its commercial genesis, a radical edge for British black music culture that has become increasingly rare due to the mainstreaming of soul and reggae in radio music programming. This situation meant that soca-calypso offered a more authentic form of black music than the commercial and white appropriations of soul. In this sense of being a critical relocation of cultural meaning and value it was considered by the station itself to be radical:

> Radical, Radical, Radical – re-notion of Connor Reeves and Anthem from last year. 'Read My Mind'. Once again it's that new hot produc- tion team on the case: Grove Chronicles. (Carnival Radio, DJ link)

Another station DJ noted what she felt to be the deep 'infinite sense of creativity and authenticity' of Afro-Caribbean music, confirming that soca offered the station and its community a radically different sound in the context of English popular music radio. Thus it clearly helped to reinvigorate the distinctiveness of black music and culture and constitute the community's 'grain of voice':

> One of the policies we are pursuing, not just going for stereotypical soul which is now become pop at any rate, diggin' much deeper into that infinite source of creativity which is black music. (Carnival Radio, DJ link)

Soca also helped to present an alternative to the co-option of soul and reggae (seen once as the 'protest music *par excellence*' in Britain (Denselow 1989: 128) in the context of the radio field. Soca also filtered into the station's concern to appear to share the populist values of mainstream radio and to different generations:

> There was sort of a mixture where soca-calypso being the minority in this case, generally speaking inner-city-wise it's mainly soul then reggae then soca, but for the older generation it's soca first then soul and reggae. So it sort of went from some shows that were mainly soca to the mainstream of the shows which were soul, reggae and soca mixed in as well. (Carnival Radio)

Thus the 'grain of voice' of soca-calypso music helped resolve a number of concerns and competing pressures on the station. It met the desire to offer a real local alternative to mainstream music pro- gramming; it served to broaden the local inner-city appeal of the station across the generations; it connoted a feeling of the Caribbean and the vibrancy of its music culture, and because it was a black popular cultural form which had been neglected in Britain, it gave a distinctive 'grain of voice' in which to negotiate the parameters of symbolic power in the field of radio.

Commercial stations' mimicry of working-class voice

Sociological studies of radio are mostly characterized by ethnomethodological studies of talk radio, DJ talk or features programming (e.g. Moss and Higgins 1984; Page and Tannenbaum 1996; Scannell 1991; Zelizer 1993). However, as in other areas (such as in telephone communication – see Chapter 8) these studies of linguistic exchange in radio talk fail to address the social role that accent and dialect play in radio. Voice has been defined in this chapter as acting to project a group's identity and negotiate a position in the field. But in contrast to the commercial and state forces shaping the field of radio, the dominance of RP in high culture and other elite zones of the cultural field, popular music radio is actually one of the few institutions of the media where working-class voice has attained something of a dominant position. However, this feeling of its being an institution-alization of a working-class voice in mainstream radio is actually only apparent and highly ambiguous because it has little relationship to any identifiable community or interests within the broad cultural spectrum which is the working class at any one time.

Rather, radio 'mimics' working-class speech by a type of 'bi-vocal' discursive structure. Bi-vocality institutes a very powerful position for the DJs, 'hosts' or presenters who can assume a number of different voices in order to engage with their socially heterogeneous audiences. Mimicry like this can be seen as a 'strategy of condescension' (Lipi-Green 1998: 208) and, as Montgomery notes, where their empowered voice briefly appropriates a dialect or accent:

> As listeners we are constantly made aware of other (invisible) elements in the audience of which we form a part. At the same time, however, the discourse does not speak from a single authoritative position. It is sutured out of fragments which allow one 'voice' to put itself at a distance from, or call into question, the other voices present in its composition. (Montgomery 1986: 438)

Other voices that appear beside the DJ or host as a result of this tend to come across as appellant or subordinate. In mainstream talk radio, the institutional voice takes up this position by usually going second in order to counter lay arguments. The outcome is the imposition of symbolic violence and the reinforcement of the divide between 'those who are entitled to express opinions and those who are entitled to experiences' (Scannell 1989).

Commercial and regulatory pressures also highly mediate the appearance of any distinctive working-class voice in popular music stations. Such stations have to appeal to both a mass audience and advertisers and, as a result, any really locatable, 'knowable' working-class community comes second to these concerns. Preferring not to be associated with any particular, recognizable, local accent commercial stations will often use a presenter with an accent from an area that is well out of the station's coverage. Thus, of two of the prominent DJ personalities in a major commercial station in the area one was a Scottish 'shock jock' and the other was Noddy Holder, ex-lead of the group Slade, who is from Birmingham – over sixty miles away. This allows shock jocks to insult particular segments of the local audience – for example, one of these regularly makes statements such as 'everyone in Oldham is thick' (i.e. stupid) and to avoid alienating local segments of the audience.

In the following quote an executive from a major commercial station in the city makes the point that against the idea of voice or identifiable accent it is, rather, professional standards that make for good radio:

> The key to it is not accent but being able to relate to people [...] a good presenter will be able to use a kind of language that everyone will feel comfortable with.

This suggests that there is, in fact, no readily identifiable community that commercial stations actually relate to – the areas they cover are usually too large. But the need for the type of cultural distance given by using 'outsider' presenters has also to be seen in this context. UK commercial stations' transmission areas often cover audiences of around five million. So the designation of 'local' to commercial radio is in fact quite abstract, based more usually on age as the main demographic of audience identification rather than race, class or geography. This, also, actually means a very particular type of lowest common-denominator voice, referred to by one station's director as 'not doing intelligence speech but entertainment speech'.

Modification of accent is another means by which popular music radio DJs contribute to the homogenization of their, mainly, white working-class audiences. The following quote by a BBC local radio DJ (which, by the way, shows that the denigration of voice is not restricted to commercial stations alone) notes how he identifies himself as an 'ordinary working-class bloke', but decided that he needed to adopt a 'north-western accent' as a means of avoiding being identified with any particular area, social or cultural group within the region:

> [T]he reason I survived is that I have got a regional north-western accent. I haven't got a Manchester accent and I haven't got a Wigan accent. Now what having a north-western accent means for me is that what I wanted to do was get on the wireless, so I changed the way I speak and when I listen to the radio it's not me. So there is a north-west identity but it's a very large identity and it's divided between Liverpool and Manchester and then Lancashire 'pie eaters' and 'Cloggies', then posh bastards down south. So there is all that going together and the only way you can tap all of that is by being somehow north-western. But there isn't a north-western community, but they are happy to accept north-western. If I had a Salford or Wigan accent then the people of Oldham would say he's really for them, same for the people in Stockport. So it's a north-western accent.

This host's experience is common to radio presenters, whether in public-funded or commercial stations, because of the key role that RP and other forms of cultural anonymity play in creating mainstream radio's preferred form of voice:

> Most of our DJs don't have much of an accent to speak of. Our breakfast show presenter who is performing well has got a southern accent, not strong cockney or East End, a bit Thames Valley. But providing people are being entertained I don't think they care. What they don't like is strong regional accents, we know that because when we interview people with a broad accent people prefer to hear something broadcast in a much more neutral accent. (Commercial Radio Station executive)

The concern to adopt an authoritative but socially and cultural unspecific voice serves to create an imaginary, dis-located experience for the working class which contrasts to that of Carnival Radio's. DJs and presenters on Carnival Radio were relaxed about letting a local accent appear within programming because the main qualification was sharing the cultural values of the station:

> We chose the presenters initially because they had to agree to what we were doing and the way we were doing it. So you would have one show where you would have someone who speaks relatively good English and come across as a local and relate to the young people. Then the next show two hours later you would have someone who had a mix of West Indian accent communicating in the same way. (Carnival Radio)

In contrast to mainstream radio's preference for a homogeneous institutional voice, the organizers of Carnival Radio were conscious of the productivity of encounters between different cultures, and heterogeneity in speech:

> And so the culture is creeping in and a lot of it now it's such a melting pot. At the moment culture-wise as far as music media goes a lot of black culture is creeping into it, the phrases and the street song and things like that so a lot of middle class kids are using it. So it is not sort of taboo any more. So if you are interviewing someone with say a West Indian accent a lot of people would have said 'what's that he said?' But because now they hear the phrases all the time, everyday phrases, it isn't so strange any more, can tolerate it more, because you understand what they are saying. So I think that helps an awful lot where you can have people and certain entertainers who may be singing or talking in English then all of a sudden someone else in the band is doing a reggae in Jamaican accent. (Carnival Radio)

Adopting a mainstream institutional voice was not considered important for the station because it was largely self-funded and did not depend on advertising revenue. One of the station's strengths was the strong knowledge it had of its community, and of the type of music best able to give it voice. But, as we have also seen, this was a complex articulation of inner-city community and diasporic Afro-Caribbean identity. Its relaxed attitude to producing an identifiable accent accompanied the sense of self-confidence in Manchester's

Afro-Caribbean community. And, as a positively enriching cultural condition, it may well offer a model for how black British people might express themselves today, after being faced all too often in the past by the dominance of English/white culture.

We have noted above that the articulation of 'knowable' (Hall 1991) urban community and of an authentic Caribbean culture in Carnival Radio also included a reflexive awareness of the state of the field – seen in its mimicry of a mainstream mundane voice. Although constrained by state broadcasting regulations, this was turned into a strategy to gain a foothold in mainstream programming. Alongside helping us to identify lay-reflexivity, this case study also resonates with Bhabha's ideas on the contradictory nature of cultural hybridity:

> [T]he borderline engagements of cultural difference may as often be consensual as conflictual; they may confound our definitions of tradition and modernity; realign the customary boundaries between the private and the public, high and low; and challenge normative expectations of development and progress. (Bhabha 1994: 2)

Carnival Radio's grain of voice, soca-calypso music, the Caribbean dialect and the accents of its presenters mark its place in the field vis-à-vis state and commercial positions very much in this 'confounding' of 'normative expectations'.

Caribbean Carnival Radio therefore shows how in studying the field of radio voice, accent and dialect are important stakes in the struggles that take place there and make useful analytical concepts in their Bourdieusian manifestation. Observing the structural dimensions of the field, between the state, commercial and community stations, we have assessed the meaning of Caribbean Carnival's particular voice in a field-relational way. In contrast to Caribbean Carnival Radio, commercial and local BBC radio had much less connection to any real, knowable, spatially located community. Just as in the case of standardization in spoken language, any appeal by mainstream radio to particular, knowable, audiences and cultures is likely to be fundamentally bi-vocal, homogeneous and stereotypical.

7
Language, Media and Opinion Polling

This chapter develops Bourdieu's original criticisms of opinion polls (Bourdieu 1984, 1990b, 1993b) and his analysis of the political implications, and sociological meaning, of 'Don't Know' responses. Bourdieu was critical of democratic claims that polls make it possible for the working-class 'silent majority' to enter into the political field (Berinsky 2004: 8; Champagne 2005: 119) because it is they who most regularly resort to the Don't Know option. Bourdieu castigated the polling industry for its role in more general processes of symbolic violence and political domination. But he was also concerned with how polls and the mass media interact, and the role of *language* in polling discourse in marginalizing opinion 'from below'. In this respect, then, Bourdieu's ideas on polling are important in the study of the media and language.

Bourdieu's ideas also originated in the early 1970s when, as Alexander notes, concern about the language of polls and the role of the media in forming public opinion had become topical due to the Watergate crisis (Alexander 2008: 87). But by the time that Bourdieu started to become interested in polling, mid-twentieth-century journalism had developed from a news gathering to news *generating* profession. In part, newspaper polls started as a critical reaction to the dominance of polling by political parties. But by the mid-1960s 'in-house' newspaper polling culminated in developments like the partnership between the *New York Times* and CBS. This generated the first real 'flurry of strategy and tactics stories' (Mann and Orren 1992) and the 'horse race' type of reporting of election campaigns that dominates the press and media today. By the 1970s the media also took upon itself more responsibility for interpreting polling agencies' data – seen in professional developments like 'precision journalism' (Meyer 1979).

In the literature on the role of the media in 'agenda setting' there is little discussion of the actual linguistic issues involved in polls, even though there seems to be a symbiotic relationship between polls and the media:

> Pollsters rely upon news-mediated constructions of recent events, they are formulating questions not about the public's opinion in some open-ended sense, but about what the public wants to know about a situation that has already been communicatively constructed in reference to the binaries of the public sphere. (Alexander 2008: 87)

The political influence of the media is becoming more acute today because it is increasingly setting the terms for politics as politicians become no longer simply 'observers' of the media but have to give it 'observance' (Meyer and Hinchman 2002: xii).

If Bourdieu's ideas were generated at the time of these trends, he nevertheless had a highly original take on polls by exploring why working-class subjects tend to select the 'Don't Know' option more than those of other classes. For Bourdieu, Don't Knows indicate the much larger social process of symbolic violence in 'disenfranchising' working-class opinion. Bourdieu saw through one of the key ideological stances of the polling industry – that opinion 'trickles down' into society (Bourdieu and Thompson 1991: 177, 278). The Rousseauian ideas of the 'General Will' and 'rational consensus' are thus simply constructs of a political field in which polling functions to reinforce the concerns of the key forces within it – rather than the concerns of society more generally. In Bourdieu's view, the 'performativity' of polling is not that it enables pollsters to give us a true snapshot of public opinion at any one time, but rather that it 'produces' more Don't Know responses in working-class respondents than in other classes and thereby ensures their opinion will not 'count'.

As in Bourdieu's time, media and press-directed polls continuously reveal a strikingly high incidence of Don't Know responses. Polls like the March 2007 ICM/*Sunday Mirror* poll on the question of which party has the best policy on climate change has levels of Don't Knows as high as 25 per cent. The ICM/*News of the World* poll on the issue of racism in the 2008 British *Big Brother* reality TV programme has 31 per cent Don't Knows. In online polling, one of the more popular areas of polling activity today, YouGov's survey for the Scottish National Party in 2005 recorded Don't Knows at 22 per cent (on the question of whether Tony Blair 'cares about Scotland') whilst issues high on the political agenda at the time, such as Blair's policy on Iraq, also attracted 15 per cent Don't Knows. As Table 3 indicates, Don't Knows rise with more complexly worded questions, and working-class (C2DE) groups consistently have higher rates of Don't Know than other social groups.

Bourdieu thought that the language of polls, the values and attitudes expressed in them, thus bear little relevance to the lives, language and political concerns of working-class people. The problem is, then, not so much the working class's inability to form or 'to have' opinions, but that polls act to stop their expression (Berinsky 2004: 14). Bourdieu was the first to recognize the role of polls in the subordination of the working class's potentially radically counter-opinions to the dominant ideologies of that field. Symbolic violence is the '*idée force*' underlying the contemporary formation of the General Will, a violence that works on the basis of the seemingly open, yet actually exclusionary, nature of opinion polling (Bourdieu 1984: 433).

Revoicing opinion poll questions: identification bids and dispositional opinion

So Bourdieu examines Don't Knows as another aspect of the phenomenon of the working-class's 'self-censorship', the intuitive but nevertheless realistic response on their part when the political field works to exclude their opinions, experience and 'voice' (Bourdieu 1984: 417). But if Don't Knows are a form of self-censorship this is because they express a rational or 'reality principle' in the working class as it senses broader processes of discursive and linguistic exclusion/alienation from mainstream politics (Bourdieu 1984: 405).

Bourdieu sees opinion as deeply embodied in the class habitus in which attitudes and opinions derived from experience act as 'premises', in terms of linguistic dispositions and class ethos:

> The [...] principle according to which people may produce an opinion is what I call 'class ethos' (rather than 'class ethic'), by

Table 3 YouGov / *Daily Mirror* survey results

Sample Size: 2029
Fieldwork: 15th–17th October 2008

Daily Mirror

	Total	Voting Intention			Gender		Age			Social Grade		Region				
		Con	Lab	Lib Dem	M	F	18 to 34	35 to 54	55 +	ABC1	C2DE	London	Rest of South	Midlands / Wales	North	Scotland
All GB Adults	2029	676	542	224	972	1057	600	709	720	1095	932	256	653	438	501	182
Unweighted Sample	2029	675	548	221	964	1065	543	686	800	1232	795	320	647	383	499	180
	%	%	%	%	%	%	%	%	%	%	%	%	%	%	%	%
Headline Voting Intention																
Con **42**	42	100	0	0	41	43	38	44	44	47	37	46	50	45	37	18
Lab **34**	34	0	100	0	35	33	33	35	33	33	35	34	27	33	40	41
Lib Dem **14**	14	0	0	100	14	14	20	13	10	14	14	14	16	13	15	8
Other **10**	10	0	0	0	11	10	8	8	13	7	14	6	8	9	8	33
Non Voters																
Would Not Vote **7**	*7*	*0*	*0*	*0*	*6*	*8*	*11*	*7*	*5*	*6*	*9*	*5*	*8*	*7*	*9*	*7*
Don't know **14**	*14*	*0*	*0*	*0*	*10*	*17*	*15*	*14*	*11*	*14*	*13*	*11*	*12*	*20*	*14*	*7*
Irrespective of which party you yourself support how well do you think Gordon Brown has handled the financial crisis?																
Very well **16**	16	5	40	12	17	14	11	11	24	17	14	14	14	17	17	17
Fairly well **46**	46	42	51	50	49	42	45	46	46	47	44	50	44	42	46	51
Fairly badly **19**	19	27	6	18	16	22	21	22	15	20	18	20	20	21	17	18
Very badly **15**	15	22	1	16	15	15	15	16	13	12	18	10	17	15	15	10
Don't know **5**	5	4	2	4	3	7	8	5	2	5	5	6	5	5	5	6
Irrespective of which party you yourself support which team do you trust more to manage the economy successfully: Gordon Brown and Alastair Darling or David Cameron and George Osborne?																
Gordon Brown and Alastair Darling **40**	40	9	91	41	43	38	38	40	43	40	40	42	34	41	43	53
David Cameron and George Osborne **28**	28	67	2	14	28	28	25	28	30	31	24	30	35	24	25	17
Not sure **32**	32	24	8	46	29	35	37	33	27	29	35	29	31	35	33	30
Which party do you think has the best policies for protecting your family's personal economic interests?																
Conservative **31**	31	81	2	6	32	30	26	33	34	36	26	35	36	30	28	18
Labour **27**	27	3	84	11	29	26	26	27	28	26	30	27	22	27	32	36
Liberal Democrat **8**	8	2	2	52	10	6	9	8	7	9	7	7	10	8	7	10
Some other party **5**	5	1	0	1	7	4	4	5	7	4	7	5	4	3	5	15
Don't know **28**	28	14	10	31	22	34	35	27	24	26	31	26	29	32	28	22

which I mean a system of implicit values which people have internalized from childhood and from which they generate answers to very different types of questions. (Bourdieu 1993b: 152)

The dispositional-type of opinion that characterizes the working class is more diffuse and intuitive in nature and contrasts to that articulated by political parties, the middle class, and organized pressure groups:

> I have said that there is, on the one hand, mobilized opinion, formulated opinion, pressure groups mobilized around a system of explicitly formulated *interests*; and, on the other hand, there are dispositions which, by definition, are not opinion if one means by that [...] something that can be formulated in discourse with some claim to coherence. (Bourdieu 1993b: 157)

As a form of 'doxa', dispositional opinion lies unexpressed not because it is fundamentally inarticulate in nature, but due to the structure of the political field which acts to 'censor' it. We have noted elsewhere in this book, for example, how historical studies of standardization in language show that middle-class hegemony in the linguistic field works to marginalize regional accents, associated mostly with the working class. Similarly, since the 1980s in the UK there has been a reduction in the influence of working-class institutions which might have been able to offset middle-class dominance in the political field – for example, trade unions (Charlesworth 2000).

In a more detailed analysis of polls, Bourdieu argues that if working-class respondents are forced to give an opinion, if the Don't Know option is unavailable (often due to 'filters'), they will intuitively reinterpret the question in terms of their linguistic dispositions (Bourdieu 1984: 423). Bourdieu describes such responses as 'allodoxiac', indicating the way working-class respondents to polls have to 'mentally readapt' (Bourdieu 1984: 435) or 'falsely recognize' the point of a question because:

> The dominated, whose interests are bound up with the raising of consciousness, i.e. with language, are at the mercy of the discourses that are presented to them; whenever they emerge from doxa they are liable to fall into allodoxia, into all the false recognitions encouraged by the dominant discourse. (Bourdieu 1984: 461)

So the socially abstract or unfamiliar language constituting poll questions forces working-class respondents into making idiosyncratic 'readings' and reinforces the more general process of the imposition of symbolic violence that works to disenfranchise their opinion. The type of language Bourdieu is referring to can be seen in Box 1, which shows the type of socially anonymous questions making up newspaper polls. The question is posed in universalist terms, an obscuring of agency in 'some people' which sets the terms for the debate and the sectioning off of positions in respect to it.

As discussed in Chapter 3, Bourdieu's ideas on dispositional opinion, allodoxia, and his references to doxa more generally reveal the pervasive influence of Husserl's phenomenology in his work (Lane 2000; Myles 2007; Robbins 2006; Troop and Murphy 2002). Bourdieu's main preference as an 'objectivist' rather than a 'subjectivist' social scientist, is to sociologically contextualize the phenomenological ideas behind the concept of dispositional opinion, to explain its relevance in relation to the particular 'fields' in which it is deployed. Thus opinion has to be seen in relation to the political field because, in the final instance, 'in real situations opinions are forces, and relations between opinion are power relations between groups' (Bourdieu 1993b: 155).

Box 1   (YouGov/*Daily Telegraph* poll, 27–29 October 2008)

Some people say that, irrespective of how well or badly Mr Brown has handled the current crisis, he bears much of the responsibility for allowing lending and borrowing in this country to get out of hand in the first place. What is your view?

Gordon Brown bears much of the responsibility for allowing lending and borrowing to get out of hand in the first place   – 34
He bears some of the responsibility – 41
He bears very little of the responsibility – 15
He bears none of it – 3
Don't know – 8

Identification bids

But Bourdieu's reference to working-class allodoxia in relation to polls is not in order to portray it as mistaken, but to point out the critical point that pollsters' methodology needs to be more reflexive in approaching how class differences in opinion are intimately linked to social cleavages in language. Although Bourdieu indicts the social bias inherent in the language of polling, he also suggests alternative ways in which polling might be reformulated. For Bourdieu, conventional polls 'constantly beg the question' because they 'act as if they have solved the essential political question [...] the question of the transmutation of experience into discourse' (Bourdieu 1984: 460). Bourdieu argues that working-class opinion can be evoked by the use of questions which represent the views of institutions or recognized figures that embody their opinions:

> In reality, an opinion poll would no doubt be closer to what happens in reality if it were to break all the rules of 'objectivity' and give people the chance to situate themselves as they really do in real practice, that is, in relation to already formulated opinions. For example instead of asking 'Some people are in favour of birth control, others against; how about you? ...', it would provide a sense of explicit positions taken by groups mandated to establish and diffuse opinions, so that people could place themselves in relation to responses which have already been constituted. (Bourdieu 1984: 154)

Recent study in the field of behavioural research has noted how body and facial features can affect voting decisions (Little et al. 2007). However, using real groups or figures as representatives serves more to project 'idols' or 'trademarks' of opinion in polls (Bourdieu 1984: 430). This has as its closest methodological application the 'identification bid' question form (Bowler and Donovan 1998). This question form attempts to be more 'dispositional' in character, linguistically encoding opinions which make an attempt to draw links between what Bourdieu refers to as 'ethos and logos', opinions and words. In contrast, mainstream poll questions in the media generally encode factual knowledge (specific awareness of different party policies etc.) in universalistic terms. Lipari's study of the language of polls argues that, despite the inevitably conversational nature of the delivery of most polling, the formal language of polls is essentially in the 'interrogative' mode (Lipari 2000: 194). In contrast, identification bids:

> ask respondents to identify with or take a position with respect to a limited range of propositions or policy options. These questions function as a kind of pseudo plebiscite that asks respondents to select or express a preference for a given policy opinion or proposition. They also ask respondents indirectly to give voice to a statement, claim, or argument by declaring their own agreement or disagreement with a given proposition. By agreeing/disagreeing or favouring/opposing a given proposition, the respondent is doing more than simply evaluating the position, she or he is also identifying with larger social groups by adding his or her own voice or pseudo-vote to the proposition. (Lipari 2000: 203)

A key characteristic of this question form is that it is discursive (as opposed to what Lipari calls 'legislative' or 'policy' identification questions), having the 'already stated' nature Bourdieu suggests is more likely to elicit working-class opinion. Lipari argues that identification bids depend on the respondents orientating themselves less to the question/er and more to what she terms 'some vaguely derived notion of other speakers', which suggests a more sociological view of the language of opinion. Lipari gives the following question from a Princeton survey as an example:

> Now I am going to read you another *series of statements* on some different topics. *For each statement, please tell me* if you completely agree with it, mostly agree with it, or completely disagree with it:
> 'Poor people have become too dependent on government assistance programs'. (Princeton Survey Research, for *Times Mirror*, 1994) (Lipari 2000: 204)

Lipari comments that the organization of the question is such that it requests *alignment* and identification with whoever actually produced the original statement.

However, this question form does not guarantee that Don't Knows would necessarily be reduced. Take, for example, the first question in Box 2 which is an identification bid but nevertheless delivers a high percentage of Don't Knows. This is intensified in the second question, on the British Labour Party politician Peter Mandelson, even though it is using in its first bid what might be considered quite demotic language.

In the first example, all of the statements remain quite technical because they take for granted that the respondent will understand what 'free market systems' means. There has been no real engagement

Box 2   (YouGov/*Sunday Times* survey, 9–10 October 2008)

Example 1:

Which of the following statements comes CLOSEST to your view?
'Whatever the short-term problems we face today, the free market system, with its risks and rewards is the best way to increase prosperity; it would be a mistake to do anything that curbs enterprise and limits the freedom of companies, investors and employees to take their own decisions' – 20
'The free market system offers both advantages and disadvantages; the time has come to change the balance so that there is less freedom and more regulation, with the Government setting tougher rules to ensure that companies behave responsibly' – 54
'The free market system is fundamentally flawed; Britain would be more prosperous if far more companies were owned by the Government and/or their own workforce' – 12
Don't Know – 14

Example 2:

Which of these views comes closer to your own?
Peter Mandelson used to be associated with spin and sleaze. Leopards don't change their spots, so his return to government will end in tears – 50
Whatever happened in the past, Peter Mandelson is now committed to working harmoniously with Gordon Brown to ensure economic recovery – 22
Don't Know – 28

with the idea of identification bids. Instead, a type of pseudo-voice has been produced, predicated on the abstract language and an assumed knowledge about these issues that are generally of more concern to pollsters themselves as agents located in the political field.

To answer Bourdieu's criticisms the statements in identification bids must be articulated in socially appropriate linguistic forms and be consciously socially codified. To do this means sociologically mapping the various issues and forms of opinion in society rather than in the political field. Some work like this has been done by Strauss and Myers. Strauss has studied 'opinion communities' to see how opinions can be identified less individually and more in relation to issues that have 'cultural standing' or normative salience in any particular class or community:

> Opinion norms are like behavioural norms. Members of a community do not automatically follow them, but they are expected to know them, and if they deviate, to acknowledge that somehow. [...] Whether cultural standing markers are a deliberate signal or simply embedded in habitual phrasing, they can still serve as an index of cultural standing, and hence be useful for cultural analysis. (Strauss 2004: 172)

In Chapter 4, in relation to Habermas, Bourdieu's anti-Kantianism was noted. But in this case we can also note that a key reason for high incidences of working-class Don't Knows is a Kantian universalistic bias in opinion polling methodology. In seeing opinion as rationalistic pollsters fail to recognize how particular issues may or may not have socio-cultural salience. Cultural standing acts linguistically as a 'pragmatic constraint' on the articulation of opinion, and Strauss notes that 'all discourses [are] oriented toward the already uttered, the "already known" or the "common opinion" of the group' – the symptomatic 'modalities' of different social groups (Strauss 2004: 167). Similarly, Myers also notes how 'commonplaces' resulting from a group's shared experiences can act as indicators of opinion:

> Commonplaces are at the heart of legitimate public opinion – they are one way of referring to shared experiences and points of view, and affirming or questioning what we, as this group here and now, take for granted. [...] what distinguishes commonplaces from the taken-for-granted *doxa* is that they are by no means

unchallengeable; people use commonplaces as commonplaces, and happily invoke a commonplace and its opposite for the same argument, or the same commonplace for opposite arguments. (Myers 2005: 537)

These types of ideas are completely absent in the contemporary polling and media industry. But the media could start to address these points by more sociological, and linguistic, use of 'vox populi' interviews or focus groups. The data from these could then serve to publicize, articulate, the 'commonplaces', dispositional or subordinate opinion overlooked in contemporary polling. Of course, these lack the cloak of science that traditional polls have, the allure of the statistical sample, but they could actually reveal the wider reality of political opinion. Seeing, or hearing, the actual language of opinion in, say, focus groups would act to challenge the distortions of polling. Properly conducted, news media-sponsored focus groups could glean genuine political opinions and report their expression in appropriate language. The attention-grabbing nature of headlines like '4% swing to the Republicans' would not, however, be so easily generated from this type of opinion polling. But it would counter the 'irrational patterns of behaviour' that the media prompts, and instead work 'to elicit from the voters the "proper" response' (Meyer and Hinchman 2002: 64).

Bourdieu's ideas about the political implications of Don't Knows have influenced several academic studies, such as Berinksy (2004) and Althaus (2003) who make further analytical distinctions amongst Don't Knows. Berinsky argues that we need to think in terms of embodiment or 'sentiments' in which:

'wants, needs, and desires' can be thought of as the building blocks of opinions; without these underlying feelings and ideas, political cognition is not possible. (Berinsky 2004: 7–8)

Althaus notes like Bourdieu that Don't Knows indicate a 'pervasive' uneven social distribution of political knowledge (Althaus 2003: 6). This is a key factor in a system where individual opinions become aggregated into collective preferences (Althaus 2003: 4). Similarly, in a key industry manual, Schuman and Presser note that in trying to deal with Don't Knows most pollster manuals and guidance notes for interviewers advise non-acceptance (Schuman and Presser 1996: 8) or try to avoid them altogether by using 'filters'. This shows that the industry would much rather discount Don't Knows than explore their potential meaning as indicators of opinion or the repercussions that they might indicate something fundamentally wrong with polls.

The Bourdieusian idea that Don't Knows indicate a reality principle on the part of the working class is also articulated by Peterson, who notes the underlying logic of working-class awareness that 'it is not rational to be politically well-informed' (Peterson 2003: 255). Similarly, Parenti has argued that working-class apathy is rational in the face of its 'powerlessness and against being mis-led' (in (Margolis and Mauser 1989: 260). Herbst also notes the importance of Bourdieu's ideas (Herbst 2002), and contrasts lay forms of opinion to that of professional polls' 'rationalizing techniques' (Herbst 1993: 156). Herbst sees the pollsters as 'privatizing opinion' as they work to individualize, universalize and disengage opinion from its socially discrete forms of embodiment (Herbst 1993: 62–3).

The idea of voters orienting themselves to underlying, deep-seated cultural standing and identifiable figures in order to express opinion also figures in other critical literature on opinion polling (Bowler and Donovan 1998; Katznelson et al. 2002). In terms of 'voice', Berinsky (2004) has referred to the idea of 'political voice' and 'voice of the people', as well as the idea of working-class voice being left 'unspoken' or 'muted'. And Jeffrey Alexander criticizes polling in his recent book *The Civil Sphere* for its inattention to mundane speech and states that 'Collective representations of an imagined community can and must be articulated in more specific and mundane ways' (Alexander 2008: 69).

Similarly, Ginsberg argues that polls translate unformulated opinions, what Bourdieu would call dispositional opinion, into attitudes where 'in attitudinal form, opinion poses less of an immediate threat and remains amenable to modification or accommodation' (Ginsberg 1989: 281).

This chapter has used examples from polls that have been financed by print media because it is taken for granted today that the key ground for symbolic struggles over opinion takes place within the media, even if the polling institutions tend to have the monopoly of technical expertise. However, what we see reported in the media is often subject to its own news values which generally means that the 'media is forced to report only some of the results, usually without reference to the [original] words' of polls (Robinson 2001: 46). Blanchot, like Bourdieu, articulates Husserlian ideas in his criticisms of the mass mediation of public opinion which he sees as giving Kantian universalized and socially abstract opinions. The media pursues what he calls 'profound' questions that are basically 'unanswerable' and which force the masses to mimic or 'repeat' (Blanchot 1993: 18). The media thus produces:

> opinion without material basis that one reads in the newspapers – but never in any particular one – [that] is already closer to the panic character of the question. (Blanchot 1993: 19)

Blanchot is also aware of the importance of experience/dispositional opinion in offering a possible counter-force to the mass media. Dispositional opinion is seen by him as acting critically as a 'limit experience' (Blanchot 1993: 250) which, in contrast to mass-mediated public opinion, infuses everyday language with particularity or forms of judgement which challenge universality. The diffuseness of dispositional opinion remains always 'oblique' (Blanchot 1993: 238) to the abstract 'profound questioning' in opinion polls. Like Bourdieu, Blanchot sees media polls as taking ordinary language on 'a detour' as if, like the hubris of science, ordinary people were 'able to see things from all sides' (Blanchot 1993: 28).

In conclusion, in this chapter we have seen how a concern with the language of polls is an important aspect of Bourdieu's criticisms of political opinion formation. Bourdieu's sociology of language has its roots in a concern with parole rather than structure, with the socially fragmented nature of language. This position underlies his views of the need to reform polling methodology so that it articulates more accurately working-class opinion. Bourdieu's approach, particularly in the area of deploying ideas of 'dispositional opinion' and 'allodoxia' demonstrates his concern to articulate phenomenological principles into the analysis of this key aspect of symbolic power. His criticisms of the Kantian universalism that lies at the heart of mainstream opinion polling recall his debt to Husserlian phenomenology and his own view of the need for sciences like opinion polling to reflect on their own techniques and language by taking into consideration the complexities of ordinary language.

8
Bourdieu and Language Technologies: Texting–Mobility–Habitus

This chapter revisits the theoretical debates discussed in Chapter 3. However, this concern is pursued in relation to a discussion of the linguistic and cultural debates about the impact of the mobile telephone on language. By following Bourdieu's concern with language as embodied practice, and something that can be analysed in relation to the twin dimensions of field and practice, this chapter presents an alternative approach to understanding the relationship between 'language technologies' and society. In essence, Bourdieu gives a critical position from which to counter the universalizing accounts of language and technology which characterize ethnomethodology and postmodernist studies. Also discussed are sociolinguistic accounts of mobility and medium theory, which together offer additional theoretical perspectives that have some affinity with Bourdieu's.

As with the media more generally, significant and new developments in communication technologies are likely to affect the 'system of relations' that characterize the field, the 'standing' positions between different social forces. In contrast to much of this book, however, where we have noted how the powerful have dominated discursively (such as in polling), in regard to mobile telephony and text messaging it is generally recognized that young working-class people seem to have endowed it with most significance in terms of lifestyle. Concern about text messaging affecting Standard English, the street theft of mobiles, the 'happy slapping' phenomenon in the UK (in which camera-phones are used to record assaults on people in public places) are indications of how the working class is both positively and negatively associated with mobile telephony.

This association suggests that the mobile's 'artefactual' significance for this group might point to deeper issues about relations of symbolic power and language, rather than simply those of consumer habits or prestige. As Russell's research notes, in the Paris riots of 2005 mobile phones and text messaging were the 'preferred frontline communication medium of the rioters and young residents of the banlieus (the working class suburbs)' (Russell 2007: 290).

Since 2005 class issues in academic studies of mobile telephone use have been somewhat sidelined due to the pervasiveness of the technology across all classes. But this is a serious neglect because it means that the cultural-class relationship in mobile technology also gets overlooked – as if generality of access to a technology therefore means similarity of use. As there has been hardly any academic research into the class dimensions of mobile phone use (and even less about how digital textual forms like SMS (short message system) may also be differentiated in use by class) the following sections therefore develop theoretical arguments from Bourdieu's position in order to suggest ways in which we can understand the class dimensions of language and mobile phone technology.

In terms of relations of symbolic power the way in which working-class users of mobile telephony and text messaging have appropriated this technology act as a point of engagement with the dominance of Standard English in the linguistic field. Indications of this can be seen in the periodic 'moral panics' over the effect of text messaging on standards of English, the idea of 'verbal contagion' (Jones and Schieffelin 2009: 1050) as identified in the following quotes:

> But teachers report that their biggest headache is text language. One pupil wrote in a piece of work 'I noe u dnt noee mii, I donno huu u r', which translates as 'I know you do not know me, I don't know who you are'. One respondent said: 'Pupils had forgotten how to write as they spent so much time texting.' (*Daily Mail*, 12 December 2008)

> Many GCSE English students did not realise that phrases such as 'get off of' and 'she was stood' were grammatically incorrect. It comes amid fears that the use of social networking websites and mobile phone text messaging is undermining children's literacy skills. [...] Only 41 per cent realised that an adjective had been used in place of an adverb in the phrase 'come quick'. Fewer

than six-in-10 pupils correctly identified 'off of', 'she was stood' and 'this man showed us' as ungrammatical. (*Daily Telegraph*, 24 October 2008)

However, the issues that arise due to mobile telephony and text messaging go beyond the assumption of these reports that it is simply a problem of age, or generation. We need to see how the impact of mobile telephony and text messaging on language provokes deeper issues about processes involved when language technologies are appropriated by more popular, demotic, forces 'from below'.

Mobile SMS text messaging was developed in the early 1990s as an alternative to pagers, but it took off in 2001 when it was first fully developed commercially. SMS as a mobile technology can be distinguished from 'instant messaging' (IM) and 'Twitter' which are mainly internet-based forms of social networking, allowing their users to simultaneously send and receive messages from and to a large number of recipients. In contrast, text messaging and mobile telephony have had a dynamic effect on people's ability to overcome the spatio-temporal restrictions on their lives, at least to the extent of being able to maintain contact with home and family. Mobile technologies like SMS have been seen more generally in terms of facilitating an 'imaginary' form of space in which young people, mainly, experience co-presence outside the constraints of adult space (Baron 2008). Young people are seen as the chief beneficiaries of the 'affordances' deriving from the asynchronicity of the technology, allowing them to negotiate intimacy 'at a distance'. Text messaging has also been seen as undermining the need for some of the common 'formalities' associated with most other forms of human communication, for example 'openings' and 'closings' in conversational exchanges (Spagnolli and Gamberini 2007).

Linguistics-based accounts

Linguistics-based studies of mobile telephony and SMS examine the 'functional' and stylistic dimensions of text messaging. They look at how the typographic innovations associated with text messaging are indications of quite normal processes, the internally driven characteristics found in language change and development. Thus Crystal's linguistics-based approach to text messaging (2008b) deploys universalist ideas developed by him in relation to computer-mediated communication (CMC), the internet, 'netspeak' and related developments in digital language technologies such as email (Crystal 2001). In the early to mid-1990s any thought of using more considered sociological distinctions seemed to be irrelevant as postmodern ideas of 'cyber culture' and 'online communities' (Rheingold 2000) became the norm. CMC was seen as a hybrid, specialized internet language allowing 'communication in situations where neither speech nor writing can easily substitute' (Baron 2000: 259). As Jones and Schieffelin note, linguistics-based approaches study the style of text messaging in terms of a 'discrete but generalizable set of generative rules and maxims' (Jones and Schieffelin 2009: 1051). In their own work, therefore, Jones and Schieffelin argue that texting is now influencing the patterns of everyday speech (Jones and Schieffelin 2009: 1052). But in Crystal's early work on CMC bold claims were made for the radical impact of the net on language (Crystal 2001). Crystal, as an anti-prescriptivist, sees language as an ever-changing organism which undermines the rules established by grammarians. Language therefore naturally changes due to the intersection of its internal dynamics and interaction with social and technological developments. In relation to text messaging Crystal argues similarly that it is fundamentally a normal practice of language, abbreviations occurring in only around 10 per cent of all messages and most of these have an established history (Crystal 2008a). He refers in this respect to Swift's comment on the 'barbarous custom' of abbreviation in the eighteenth century and the commonplace nature of 'deviant spellings', such as 'wot' and 'cos'.

What Crystal does find novel in text messages, however, is the combination of abbreviations and 'full words':

> There are no less than four processes combined in iowan2bwu 'I only want to be with you' – full word and an initialism and a shortened word and two logograms and an initialism and a logogram. (Crystal 2008a)

Alongside these lexical and stylistic innovations associated with texting, writers in this area also note other aspects of mobile use – such as clandestine messaging between students in classrooms. Baron (2008) and Crystal (2008b) make much of the supposedly 'cryptic' aspects of the language of text messages. Before the advent of 'free text message' deals by mobile phone companies (which allow unlimited use of texts so that users can simply carry on any one message into another), the 160 character restriction of SMS was seen as leading to pervasive use of numeric-phonic rebuses such as 'L8'. Rebuses indicate an important source for the oralized and phoneticized spellings, and letter–number homophones found in SMS messaging.

Although linguistics approaches help in identifying the 'formal' features and linguistic determinations of text messaging, this is not enough to explain the variations arising from use or the cultural and class dimensions in symbolic power struggles. Due to the highly phonetic-nature of text messaging and its characteristically compressed and disjunctive nature, it is often referred to as 'text-speak'. So, even though as a form of digital print medium its spelling and grammar should be more standardized in character than in spoken language, it actually approximates the more informal qualities of 'small talk'. From a Bourdieusian approach and its focus on language at the level of 'parole', this is a critical characteristic of text messaging, suggestive of a practice where the demotic and dynamic aspects of agency in language might be freed.

Medium theory

Throughout this book we have noted that Bourdieu's account of language stresses its embodied aspects – as practice, but that he has been criticized for this by linguistics-based approaches. It is argued that the 'internal' determinations of a language as a form of technology – for example, the particular constraints that arise from its print or textual forms – are overlooked by Bourdieu. However, the more fruitful area to engage with this kind of argument, the idea of language having its own determinations as a technology, is not really in linguistics, but in the medium theory associated with McLuhan (1967), Ong (1982) and the Toronto School. This school points to historical trends in language technologies such as the printing press, the telegraph, and the mass media as a whole, as influencing the form (and sometimes the content) of language. A common example used to support this argument is that of the Chinese pictogram writing system. This is able to represent multiple regional dialects and consonant and vowel sounds with ease, whereas alphabetic systems are highly restricted in comparison, stimulating standardization and rationalization more generally, and creating the problem of 'marking' of regional accents as a consequence. McLuhan saw the invention of print as suppressing the more phatic or gestural nature of its historical precedents such as the ideogram/pictographic writing systems of the Euphrates delta (although he also saw the ideogram as a key rebus in the development of the phonetic alphabet (McLuhan 1967: 35). The rise of print culture in Europe was, in McLuhan's view, a technological 'extension' of our sense of sight. These technologies were also 'hot' and served to transform the social relations that obtained in earlier more traditional or 'colder' societies:

> Only the phonetic alphabet makes such a division in [our] experience, giving its user an eye for an ear and freeing him from the tribal trance of resonating word magic and the web of kinship. (McLuhan 1967: 93–5)

McLuhan and the Toronto School presented their arguments in a technological determinist, and by implication, universalizing way. Although strong in depicting large-scale historical changes and variations in languages as a result of developments in 'writing systems' and print technologies, the Toronto School did not think much about how different class groups may be implicated in these changes and in different ways.

So the Toronto School might well interpret the use of supplementing icons, ideograms (i.e. symbols which represent a word by a picture (e.g. two legs to represent the word 'walking'; Harris 1986: 32), and pictograms or 'Smileys' in text messaging as signalling a potentially new direction in print culture as it becomes digitalized and as access to print becomes more democratic. But these arguments can be reconsidered, however, in relation to symbolic power struggles. In this respect, we can see how the resort to the various forms of rebuses in text messaging suggests that core issues about the very nature, the 'character', of written and textual linguistic forms is at stake. Text messaging has the character of the informality, fluidity, we expect of language as 'parole', a ludic quality, which prompts its users to escape from the historically relative strictures of standardization. But in contrast to McLuhan, we can interpret the 'paralinguistic' nature of text messaging as a demotic impulse, a desire by ordinary people and, more particularly, the young working class, to 're-embody' print and get it closer to signifying the informal, non-standardized, class, registers of speech. The embodied nature of language, usually seen simply as an aspect of facial and gestural expression, or metalinguistic functions of intonation and 'voice', can be seen as inspiring the highly phoneticized language of text messaging.

Seeing text messaging in this way reminds us of how written language evolved from the rebus, and that there is always the potentiality that the suppressed social impulse to re-embody print, and language technologies more generally, might resurface. Smileys and other emoticons in text messaging therefore symbolize much more – the highly socially variable 'kinesics' of oral language that originally impelled proto-written language forms like pictographs, and spoken language. The dependency of the meaning of the spoken word on context and accompanying indexical signs such as gestures, is therefore partially mimicked in digital text forms like SMS where idiosyncratic symbols and phonetic spellings are oriented to particular receivers. In this Bourdieusian formulation, then, we can recognize texting as a technological example of the ever-present dynamic of language in its 'practical' state to break out of its standardized boundaries. As Jones and Schieffelin state:

> [T]he verbal ingenuity associated with texting – and talking text – should be viewed not as evidence of linguistic decline, but rather in terms of the reflexive, metalinguistic, sophistication it necessarily presupposes and potentially promotes. (Jones and Schieffelin 2009: 1075)

Although not in themselves making a class-based argument, Jones and Schieffelin nevertheless argue that 'textese' discussions on YouTube, provoked by verbal hygienists' reactions to its invasion in mainstream TV advertisements, are 'at times talking text *and* talking back to language prescriptivists' (Jones and Schieffelin 2009: 1075).

Bourdieu, language and technology

Although Bourdieu has discussed and analysed the status of the natural sciences in many of his works (Bourdieu 2004) he did not pay much attention to technology. However, in his book *Academic Discourse* he looked at educational practices as a form of technology and noted how pedagogy has to operate on the basis of particular organizations of space – such as the classroom (Bourdieu et al. 1994: 10–11). Bourdieu also discusses language as a form of technology and claims that 'apparatuses' like the academic essay are the outcome of succeeding generations of pedagogic technologies, from oral presentation to language labs (Bourdieu et al. 1994: 16–22) and that the 'rhetoric of the essay is similarly a form of linguistic technology' (Bourdieu et al. 1994: 16). Bourdieu even goes as far as to suggest new technologies may facilitate democracy in the classroom in the future (Bourdieu et al. 1994: 22).

Because of this relative neglect in Bourdieu's work, writers who have related his ideas to technological questions are relatively few. Davidson, however, underlines how Bourdieu is important in making us recognize how technologies are fundamentally social and for reminding us that what generates technology is social practice (Davidson 2004: 87). Davidson sees technology in a socially relational way – technology is always a 'positional practice' (Davidson 2004: 88) – and also recognizes that using Bourdieu can remind us to re-embody technology (Davidson 2004: 90). Thus the use of any particular communications technology, like the mobile phone, will vary due to social variations in forms of practical reason, but this must be understood in the context of the way technologies are implicated in the 'action' of all fields. Davidson thus uses Bourdieu to counter technological determinist accounts which 'dislocate' the ends and means of technologies and thereby 'disembody' them. So we need to see technological 'artefacts' or 'devices' (Davidson 2004: 90–1) like mobile phones as crucial instruments in the fields just like 'stakes' or 'actors':

> The integrity of practice is being ruptured. Social action now takes place simultaneously within a value-rich foreground of *embodied* agency and a factual, unquestionable, background of *technospheric agency*. Although Bourdieu's account of our constitution in social space neglects this rupture it is not difficult to see the importance of the dislocation of means and ends for our understanding of habitus. [...] Practical reason, stands in opposition to the dissociation of means and ends made paradigmatic in late-modern technology. The logic of practice is at odds with the logic of technology for it arises out of the generative reciprocity, or what Bourdieu calls the 'ontological complicity between the habitus and the [social field]'. (Davidson 2004: 92)

Sterne also refers to Bourdieu in his own concern to re-embody our understanding of technology. He argues that technologies are 'crystallizations of socially-organized action' (Sterne 2003) and that they act effectively as 'subsets' of the habitus or 'organized forms of movement' (Sterne 2003: 370). In reviewing the criticisms of Bourdieu for failing to theorize technology, he relates Latour's (1993) argument that Bourdieu makes the mistake of seeing technologies in an 'instrumentalist' manner (Sterne 2003: 373). However, Sterne stresses that Bourdieu nevertheless stimulates us into thinking of technological artefacts in a less 'substantialist' way – as habituated practices:

> Technologies are associated with habitus and practices, sometimes crystallizing them and sometimes promoting them. They are structured by human practices so that they may in turn structure human practices. They embody in physical form particular dispositions and tendencies – particular ways of doing things. (Sterne 2003: 377)

Such crystallizations become artefacts or, as Sterne has it 'instruments', packaged in particular ways as a result of how they are constituted in the various fields by different social groups in competitive processes of production and use.

These studies signal how it is possible to engage with technological issues about mobile telephony via Bourdieu's sociology. The idea that the mobile phone is an 'instrument' which has been appropriated by working-class users, embodied by them, resonates with these forms of arguments. In this way we can conceive of working-class affinity for mobile phone technology because it allows them to articulate 'print status' to their affinity for the more informal registers of speech. Karin Harrasser, however, criticizes social constructionist accounts such as Bourdieu's because:

> [B]y conceptionalizing technology as a kind of 'hardened' social text, these approaches tend to ignore the effects of technology on society. They do not get a good idea of the things technology does with people or demonize those effects as mere power effects already preconfigured in the social norms that determine technologies. Technodeterministic approaches (nearly all of them in the tradition of Marshall McLuhan) on the other side of the spectrum of theorizing media technologies do treat materialities

as social dispositifs. They theorize the dynamics of technological change and the consequences these changes do have on culture, society and identities. However, they cannot explain the developments of a technology other than evolutionary; technology is considered as a universal, inevitable, anthropological feature. (Harrasser 2002: 825)

Harrasser notes the superiority of social constructionist accounts to those of the Toronto School, but nevertheless seeks to overcome this divide by articulating a narratological account to these (and others like Latour/Actor Network Theory, Deleuze and Guattari and 'deterritorialization') in order to articulate how 'the "imaginary", the discursive/semiotic and techno/material are related to each other' (Harrasser 2002: 827). In contrast, Bourdieu's approach can take into account the Toronto School's arguments, particularly in relation to how language as a technology shapes human communication, but formulates these ideas in relation to symbolic power struggles. And, viewing the technology of the mobile phone as an instrument which is essentially open to articulation by either dominant or subordinate social forces means that technological artefacts like mobile phones have to be seen as embodied as a result of these processes.

But we also must see how mobiles are actually differentiated in use by social class, and this requires more sociological and empirically based knowledge. In relation to this, both Sterne and Davidson note the sociological importance of space in understanding technology – the need to think about 'placing' it (Davidson 2004: 94). However, sociological facts on SMS and mobile telephony more generally are very thin on the ground. One would think that due to the sheer volume of text messages sent per day (according to UK Mobile Trends nearly 8 billion texts were sent in the UK in May 2009 or 78.9 billion over the year – although this includes business and spam messages (Text.It 2009)) there would have been much more interest in investigating social variables in use. This is not the case, however; the research on SMS is more or less completely obsessed by age (mainly young people's use of SMS), generation, or gender differences – the over-extended sociological categories that mark sociolinguistic and postmodern approaches we will discuss below. This problem can be seen in most of the recent IPSOS-Mori surveys into technology. For example, although a 2001 report showed that 80 per cent of class ABs owned mobiles in comparison to 60 per cent of DEs, data on class in recent Technology Reports by IPSOS-Mori is no longer gathered – probably because of the more or less total social pervasiveness of mobile phone ownership. The last Family Expenditure Survey to examine mobile phone use in this way was also in 2001 when there were large disparities in ownership (Family Expenditure Survey, 2003: Chart 13.5) just before the point around 2003 where ownership took off, rising from 50 per cent of all households to 80 per cent over the following four years (Office for National Statistics Report Table 'Use of ICT at Home', March 2007).

Even during the period of the 'mobile phone divide' there had been only one or two studies which looked at class as a variable in its use. Henderson and Taylor, for example, contrast mobile phone use in a 'predominantly' white and middle-class commuter belt location with an ethnically diverse and 'deprived [public housing] estate in the north of England' (Henderson et al. 2002: 496). This longitudinal five-year study of 120 young people in two age cohorts, of 11–17- and 16–24-year-olds, found that 'particular technologies become resources in the creation of classed and gendered projects of self' (Henderson et al. 2002: 497) because:

> such practices are embedded in local cultures, shaped by class, geography, and time. The specific conditions of these young people's lives lead them to realize the potential of the mobile phone in a particular way: as a means of 'buying' forms of 'privacy and independence from parental control; of accessing social networks; and of positioning themselves within social hierarchies. (Henderson et al. 2002: 508)

They note also that Home Counties teenagers gave much less prominence to mobiles because they were generally more 'media rich' (Henderson et al. 2002: 500) than working-class users. Referring to Bourdieu, these writers thus found that the mobile phone is a prime means of generating social capital, particularly amongst working-class users. Thus, despite the mobile phone's tendency to be an 'individualizing technology', this study shows that class and other regular sociological categories are important for understanding the technology.

Another ethnographic study of mobile telephony, carried out by the UK Work Foundation, also takes issue with universalizing ideas – particularly the 'false image of mobile society' (Work Foundation 2003: 2). This study traced class and other sociological factors influencing mobile use, such as family membership position or age. Class clearly interceded at the inception of the mobile phone in the early 1990s in economic terms, when prices of phones were around £400 and thus mainly available only to higher income groups. As we have noted, at the time of the research, social disparities in ownership were still important, and they found that class groups D and E were almost 20 per cent less likely to own mobiles in comparison with Group A (Work Foundation 2003: 12). Similarly, although the importance of 'small talk' is common to all social groups, cost nevertheless was still a key factor:

> The first clear finding from our research is that money matters, and more than many commentators think. Those from highly prosperous professional backgrounds are less likely to be aware of the cost of using a phone. They won't be on prepay. (Work Foundation 2003: 33)

The Work Foundation predicted that price would continue to be an important factor due to the rise of 'advanced services (such as MMS) which are not available to pre-pay customers' (Work Foundation 2003: 47). Recent and increasingly pricey hardware developments, like Blackberries and iPhones, confirm this. However, the Work Foundation also noted that middle-income groups (earning between £17,000 and £30,000 per annum) spent significantly less on mobile telephony than those in lower income groups (Work Foundation 2003: 13) which supports the idea of the relative importance of this technology in the lives of working-class people. This is reinforced by the finding that those in the intermediate classes gave the mobile phone less significance in their lifestyle than the working class (Work Foundation 2003: 30).

Alternative explanations

Ethnomethodology and the 'affordances' of mobile phones

These sociological reports on mobile phone use and ownership serve to put some empirical data on the argument that class is an important aspect in understanding the technologizing or digitalizing of language. However, in line with this book's concern to develop the debate initiated by Bourdieu in his criticisms of ethnomethodology, interactionism and sociolinguistics, as well as the implied criticisms of postmodernism and CDA, the following sections outline some of the arguments on mobile telephony from these perspectives. We will look firstly at ethnomethodological studies of mobiles and then go on to postmodernist and sociolinguistic studies. Although all of these approaches signally fail to consider class, they nevertheless have generated some important data on certain aspects of mobile phone use and text messaging habits.

The key focus of the ethnomethodological and conversational analysis approach is to explain how mobile phones impact on everyday communication. This approach recognizes that the social uses of technology have distinct social causes, but the distinctive problem is to account for how any communications technology such as the mobile phone will have certain 'affordances' which both enable and restrict practice. However, CA approaches nearly always remain blind to power and class as factors in communication, and this seems particularly the case in relation to texting or in the language and technology relationship more generally.

In an ethnomethodological study of text messaging of young adults in Italy, Spagnolli and Gamberini explore how universal structures of conversation, such as 'adjacency pairs' and 'sequentiality', might be influenced by the particular affordances of SMS. Due to the informality of SMS they found that openings and closing were less significant than in face-to-face communication, or in ordinary landline telephony because the phone identifies the name of the sender of the incoming text (Spagnolli and Gamberini 2007: 349–51). However, whilst 'adjacency pairs' might be modified by texting (Spagnolli and Gamberini 2007: 351–3) turn-taking retains its normal pattern:

> The turns of the person who initiates the exchange are likely to be reciprocated, whereas the turns of the recipient are likely to conclude the exchange. (Spagnolli and Gamberini 2007: 355)

They account for this by restating the standard ethnomethodological understanding of the positions of sender–receiver relations in the 'action sequence'. So whilst stressing the particular affordances of

SMS, they nevertheless argue that this cannot account for how most messages still rely on 'existing conversational practices':

> Strategies to deal with spatiotemporal constraints do not merely consist of 'abbreviations' and 'simplifications': they rely on partici-pants' ability to recognize what is implicit and what is expectable. (Spagnolli and Gamberini 2007: 360)

Spagnolli and Gamberini also note how 'formality' in conversational exchange in normal telephone conversation, such as the need for salutations, is generally abandoned in text messaging:

> Starting and ending an SMS encounter without openings and closures is, then, a practice that exploits the technical affordances of the medium in a socially significant way: the interlocutors treat them-selves as being already available in the communicative sense, their mediated presence being ceaseless in what has been termed as a 'sense of perpetual contact'. (Spagnolli and Gamberini 2007: 351)

A problem arises, however, with exploring how formality may have changed due to text messaging when only looking at communica-tion between peers, as this research does. Obviously, the formality or not of text messaging needs to be explored in relation to a number of other social axes, such as texts sent between teacher and student, or employer–employee, an obvious power dimension of the practice characteristically ignored in this approach.

In another ethnomethodological study of telephony, Hutchby directly engages with Gibson's idea of 'affordances' (Gibson and Pick 2000) and the social uses of technology. Hutchby attempts to fuse con-versational analysis and the idea of affordances to show that, just as in conversation there is a specificity of meaning in distinct contexts, so language technologies have a 'whatness', an indexicality of meaning in 'occasioned' settings (Hutchby 2001: 23). But where Gibson stresses the 'system of possibilities' (Hutchby 2001: 32) of technologies, how they must necessarily constrain our ability to socially shape them, Hutchby argues that they are chiefly subject to modification in social practices (Hutchby 2001: 13–26). These practices, however, are highly normative (Hutchby 2001: 181) in character – the classic regularities of conversational exchange focused on by CA.

Hutchby also looks at the 'behavioural' (Hutchby 2001: 59) and observable aspects of people's use of the telephone. Hutchby does this in order to counter Woolgar's more abstract 'computational' approach which he sees as falling into the mistake of 'attributing plans' (Hutchby 2001: 138) to potential users. Hutchby is also critical of Grint and Woolgar's idea of the 'discursive shaping' of technology which he sees as drifting too far away from understanding the 'intrinsic properties of technology' (Hutchby 2001: 23–4). In contrast, Hutchby notes Schutz's view of how we continually make sense of the interactional situations we find ourselves in, the constant monitoring of our behaviour. He argues that this concern should be applied to analysing the particular role that technological artefacts might have in such situations (Hutchby 2001: 41). He therefore modifies the assumption in CA of the socially determining role of 'competences' in language, showing how these may well be *disabled* by, for example, computer-mediation of conversation:

> The communicative affordances of such devices may enable the ascription of competence, but they also disenable many of the degrees of competence that are bound up with the management of basic interactional routines. (Hutchby 2001: 171)

In this context, Hutchby also refers to Harvey Sacks' idea of the 'next turn as proof procedure' in order to understand the particular ordering of telephone conversations. Hutchby notes how the strategies used by 'cold callers' such as 'voice samples' allow them to avoid the usual formalities of announcing who they are (Hutchby 2001: 108).

The key problem with the ethnomethodological account of language and technology is that it fails to consider how talk is conditioned by cleavages such as social class. Focusing on observational data means that the conditioning of participants' roles by these forces and relations in the linguistic field is overlooked. This conditioning may not be immediately obvious to the participants, but even where they most obviously are, for example if regional accents become thematized by the actors during the 'constant monitoring' of conversation, ethnomethodologists would not be able to account for it. For all of its highly detailed coding schemes for indicating gaps and stresses in conversational exchange, CA does not have a code for accents and similar paralinguistic aspects of conversation. And when one considers how accent matters in the location decisions for call centres, understanding the politics of language at the level of 'parole' means that it has, nevertheless, repercussions that suggest it should be given the status of 'serious speech'.

Postmodern accounts – power to the 'people'

A similar indifference to social class underlies postmodern accounts of mobile telephony. For example, Urry argues that the mobile phone facilitates temporal 'connectivity' and 'fluidity' so that 'perpetual gossip at-a-distance helps people live in fragmented worlds' (Urry 2007: 175). This approach argues that traditional notions of place-based language communities become outmoded by identities which are 'more engendered through relations made and sustained on the move, in liminal "interspaces"' (Urry 2007: 177). Urry argues that 'space age' time and space defuses the older coordinates of mass society (such as GMT; Urry 2007: 175) to facilitate the contemporary time of mobs, tribes and connections based on identities that surpass class, region or other older sociological coordinates.

Fortunati (2002), similarly, argues that traditional sociological categories now require redefinition in the face of mobility. He argues that the multimedia nature of the mobile has de-differentiated text and speech, and changes 'reality in its widest sense, or its social representation' (Fortunati 2002: 513). Fortunati sees the mobile as an individualizing technology, one which dramatically privatizes public space but also 'reinforces profane space' (Fortunati 2002: 516–20). The public sphere thus becomes redefined as mobiles strengthen the private sphere (unlike land-lines with precise locations) or at least allow greater control to the user as to who she or he wishes to be in contact with. Fortunati also argues that the role of the mobile as a status symbol is now outdated – its principal status being as a 'citizenship commodity' (Fortunati 2002: 523).

The mobile phone industry is very much under the sway of postmodern academic perspectives. For example, TalkTalk's Digital Anthropology report argues that 'Social networking will replace social class as the main determining factor in people's economic well-being' (TalkTalk 2008: 1075). The TalkTalk research classifies mobile phone users into six 'tribes' and also comes up with a universal concept of 'Homo Digitalis'. A similar industry report based on postmodern principles was produced by Sadie Plant for Motorola. This gathers empirical observation data of the street behaviour of people using mobile phones and focuses on the bodily demeanour of mobile phone users and the

> [v]ariations in the ways in which peoples' eyes respond to a mobile call. Some mobile users adopt the scan, in which the eyes tend to be lively, darting around, perhaps making fleeting contact with people in the vicinity, as though they were searching for the absent face of the person to whom the call is made. (Plant 2001: 53)

Plant refers to the 'Keitai' in Japan as exemplifying a mobile generation in which 'thumb culture' has started to have recursive effects on other habits. The report argues that young people's thumbs are now so conditioned by texting that it is starting to replace the forefinger as the primary digit – 'they even point at things and ring doorbells with their thumbs' (Plant 2001: 53). Plant underlines how this generation is attracted to the mobile's affinity to 'virtual' relationships in which 'friendships involve constructed personalities and sometimes complex webs of multiple personas and duplicitous affairs' (Plant 2001: 29). Due to the observational and behavioural focus of this research, Plant categorizes mobile users in terms of how they appear to use phones, rather than in relation to pre-standing social classifications (Plant 2001: 34–6) (although she does examine broad gender differences in users; Plant 2001: 42–3). She describes six types of mobile 'characters' and coins names for them such as the 'swift talker' and 'chattering sparrow' (Plant 2001: 66). Plant does argue that the key independent causal force affecting phone use is in location and environment which condition either discreet or overt uses of mobiles (Plant 2001: 38–9). She argues that location and environment 'dictate' mobile manners and that these can 'change according to mood, location, and the nature of a call the relation it involves' (Plant 2001: 66).

Rheingold refers appreciatively to the Motorola research and similarly argues that mobile phones enable individuals to 'move out' of present company and space and inhabit two contexts more or less at the same time. But just how mobile technologies become socially energized in locations requires us to consider the role of 'smart mobs':

> Smart mobs might also involve yet-unknown properties deriving from the dynamics of situations, not the heads of actors.

Goffman's interactional order, the social sphere in which complex verbal and non-verbal communications are exchanged among individuals in real time, is precisely where individual actions can influence the action thresholds of crowds. (Rheingold 2002: 175)

Mobile communications thus allow 'public flocking' behaviour of various tribes (Rheingold 2002: 13), enabling new forms of assembly for teenagers as time becomes 'softened' (Rheingold 2002: 5). Although Rheingold generally does not consider the class dimensions of 'mobs' (as Russell (2007) does), he does refer to how Hip Hop culture teenagers 'favour' 'Motorola's two way pagers, whilst young stockbrokers, suits and geeks in the information technology industry favour the Blackberry' (Rheingold 2002: 23). The way this comes across seems to see cultural and economic constraints as 'choices'.

Plant points positively to the etymological roots of 'mobile' in terms of 'mobile vulgus' – the 'excitable crowd' (Plant 2001: 31). But 'people', 'crowd' and 'mob' are in actual fact sociologically vacuous, as are other common focuses such as 'generation' (Goggin 2004). Generation is particularly favoured by Rheingold and his concern with 'thumb culture' and texting 'tribes'. Due to this, postmodern accounts never really break out of the preconstructed bases of understandings about the relationship between language and technology and thereby fail to account for how power might influence this relationship.

Sociolinguistic studies

Sociolinguistic studies of mobile technology tend to be case studies examining gender and age variables in mobile use with a veritable host of studies of school and university students. Sociolinguists ignore class in mobile telephony because, unlike land-line phones, the mobile is seen as having an 'individualizing' impact on communication (Ling 2004). Ling and Yttri, for example, in a comparative study of three different age groups, have examined how mobiles are used to facilitate 'micro-coordination' in everyday life. They found that a form of 'hyper-coordination' was a particular feature of teens' mobile use because the asynchronicity of texting allows them to 'arrange face' (Ling and Yttri 2002: 159). Similarly, Ling and Baron undertook a 'corpus-based' analysis of the features of text messages (such as abbreviations and emoticons) used by students at an American Midwest university and found more use of emoticons in text messages as against instant messages (IM) (Ling and Baron 2007). Another similar study is Green's which looks at 16-year-old schoolchildren and finds that texting functions as a form of gift-exchange requiring complex rituals of reciprocation (Green 2003: 209).

Kasesniemi and Rautiainen undertook a thousand thematic qualitative interviews with teenagers on the topic of text messaging. They asked the teenagers to save their messages and the research then focused   on the interviewees' own classifications (Kasesniemi and Rautiainen 2002: 175). They found more collective forms of mobile texting use – such as chain texts, message collecting and collective reading, which 'goes against the image of mobile communication as an individualistic communication channel' (Kasesniemi and Rautiainen 2002: 181). The teens also showed plenty of creative innovation in their use of abbreviations and spelling and grammatical variation (Kasesniemi and Rautiainen 2002: 184). Thus, they found that 'best friends and acquaintances [...] receive messages laced with slang, plays on local dialects, puns and insider vocabulary' (Kasesniemi and Rautiainen 2002: 185).

In one of the more extensive sociolinguistic studies of text messaging, Thurlow (like Hutchby) considers SMS in relation to the idea of 'affordances'. Thurlow notes four such affordances – transportability, adaptability, affordability and quietness-discretion (Thurlow 2002/3: 15). Thurlow argues that the high use of abbreviations in text messaging is less the result of technological constraints and due more to 'discursive demands such as ease of turn-taking and fluidity of social interaction'. Thurlow also classifies the content of texts in terms of their 'communicative functions' (relational and informative) which he sees as prompting changes in language register (Thurlow 2002/3: 17). As in Ling and Yttry, the affordance of texting's asynchronicity gives its users 'time for reflection'. SMS also enables a 'more informal register' in typography which derives in turn from the more general importance of small talk in human interaction (Thurlow 2002/3: 28). Thurlow is critical of writers like Kasesniemi and Rautiainen for over-hyping the linguistic innovations of text messaging. In his examination of 544 text messages sent by 159 'older teenagers' (first year university students) he notes how they served:

[t]he sociolinguistic maxims of (a) brevity and speed, (b) paralinguistic restitution and (c) phonological approximation, young people's

messages are both linguistically unremarkable and communicatively adept. (Thurlow 2002/3: 1)

Thurlow thus found abbreviations figuring in only 18.75 per cent of the messages whilst there were very few letter–number homophones. But there was frequent use of apostrophes (35 per cent). In contrast to Kasesniemi and Rautiainen, Thurlow found only limited use of chain messages and 'friendship maintenance' was the largest function (23 per cent).

Although seemingly more grounded in empirical research of defined social groupings, sociolinguistic studies have totally overlooked class as a variable in use of SMS or mobile telephony more generally. Little attempt has been made to take stock of broader socioeconomic differences within the preferred focus of this approach on students and teenagers. Because a more sociologically refined basis to this research is missing, questions of symbolic power in the area of text messaging thus become obscured. The apparent grounding in empirically delineated groups that marks this approach is, therefore, actually quite superficial and shares many of the a-sociological characteristics of postmodern approaches.

Conclusion

In this chapter we have seen how Bourdieu's practice-based account of language and technology can be allied with elements of medium theory to present a class analysis of the impact of the mobile phone and SMS messaging on language. This chapter has argued that text messaging is closer to the informality of speech than print or text, and this enables its articulation in, and affinity to, working-class lifestyle more readily than in the middle class. The popularity of the mobile phone and its symbolic importance in working-class life indicates that language technologies can, occasionally, be appropriated by the less powerful in modern societies.

Conclusion: Linguistic Market, Audiences and Reflexivity

This conclusion discusses four questions arising from the foregoing study of language and the media. Firstly, because Bourdieu's ideas on language were conceived of quite some time ago (principally in the 1970s), one might ask whether they are still relevant to theoretical debates on language and the media today. Secondly, it may also be asked why certain concepts from Bourdieu's theoretical repertoire have been subordinated in this book. This relates in particular to the idea of linguistic 'market', which has only really been discussed in formal terms in Chapters 1 and 3. Thirdly, even if this study has been focused mainly on the 'internal' relations of the media field, what of the reception and audience dimensions of this topic? Fourthly, if it is accepted that reception is indeed a subordinate concern of the foregoing analysis, to what extent can the postulation of a Husserlian review of Bourdieu (the third of this book's key themes) be sustained if we have not 'heard' the voices of lay actors themselves?

In relation to the first point, at many points in this book Bourdieu's confrontation with structuralism has been expressed in theoretical terms (Chapters 1 and 3) and in relation to Barthes's semiotics in the analyses of practices of radio and photojournalism in Chapters 5 and 6. When Bourdieu was originally engaged in these debates he was very much acting against the high tide of the influences of structuralist analyses in anthropological (Lévi-Strauss), political ('structural Marxism') and textual (Barthes) manifestations. Today, following the increasing sophistication of post-structuralist and postmodern analyses, the theoretical issues have moved on from the concerns over the 'analogonic' nature of the photograph (due in no small part to digital photography) or the problem of synchronicity of structuralist explanations of practice addressed by Bourdieu in *Outline of a Theory of Practice*.

But the chapters on photography, polling and text messaging have pitted Bourdieu's ideas against more contemporary and more sophisticated accounts – particularly in relation to postmodernism. In Chapter 8 on text messaging the increasing phoneticization of digital-delivery of language was seen to challenge standardization – giving status to 'mundane textual' (Kress 1997) practices. Whatever the merits of postmodern arguments about this being a 'time of tribes', and Derrida's confabulations of text and speech in *On Grammatology* (that the distinct origins of written language mean it has its own dynamics and possibly recursive effects on spoken language itself), class analysis can nevertheless present another dimension to these contemporary questions. In any case, when it comes to questions of *language* and the media there is still a need to consider Saussurian structuralist linguistics because it remains an important influence, particularly in respect to the underlying Hallidayian precepts of linguistics-based approaches like CDA. The sharp debates in the pages of *Linguistics and Education* (Hasan 1999a) stemming from the publication of the English translations of Bourdieu's essays on language shows that structuralism is still very influential in academic linguistics today.

Similarly, one recurrent issue in this book has been to show how Bourdieu's countering of structuralist arguments on language (by stressing 'parole') has real analytical weight in contrast to the dismissal of this by writers like Hasan. The concern with the language of polls as verbal practice (in their actual delivery by 'door-step' interviewers) is the basis of Bourdieu's criticisms and recommendations for 'identification bids' questions. Similarly, in relation to text messaging, by underlining the variations in the phoneticization of messages, 'text speak', Bourdieu's underlying respect for the ever-present ability of lay and working-class subjects to break out of the constraints of standardization informs the analysis.

One area of Bourdieu's approach which has not been elaborated in any great detail in this book has been his idea of the 'linguistic market'. But the market itself has a somewhat problematic status in his work, particularly when we consider what Russell refers to as the increasing tendency in the modern media to blur the lines of production and consumption (Russell 2007). Bourdieu himself notes that it has at least two meanings in his work, as indicating economic value and as a mechanism of exchange, and Chapter 3 also noted Chouliaraki and Fairclough's critical comments in this respect (Chouliaraki and Fairclough 1999: 104). We have also noted in Chapter 1 how it is hard, particularly in the case of language and the media, to separate out the internal and external areas of the market when agents in the field of journalism are seen as more important than grammarians or linguistics dons in setting the standards of usage. The idea of the market suggests relational values of the positions in the linguistic field and how these might be enhanced or diminished in the media field, but much of the time the idea of social status as attached to different registers of language seems to be of more importance, i.e. the more established sociological metaphor of hierarchical order.

In relation to the third issue, I am conscious that it could be argued that a missing element in this study has been audiences and reception. Indeed, Benson's work has the merit of linking production and consumption in the media field in this way (Benson 2006). However, my concern in the chapter on radio with how different views can be associated with different positions *within* the media field, of production, indicates how this can be articulated with the kind of theoretical exposition of Bourdieu's ideas characterizing most of the studies contained in this book. One area where clear statistical data on media consumption is easily available is in media viewing and newspaper audience reports to the industry (e.g. the Rajar organization in the UK). However, beyond its role in perhaps helping to 'plot' the lines of the field at any one time, I do not consider this data as having any fundamental bearing on issues of language and symbolic power in the media. In any case, there is always the question of where, or at what 'level' (i.e. 'micro', 'meso' and 'macro'), the sociological 'break' from actors' own opinions is going to be made. Essentially this book has leant towards the textual, seen as parole, as the 'expression' of deeper determinations arising from the structure of the social field.

Such questions in relation to reception are perhaps also provoked by the ethnomethodological position, particularly in the area of methodological approaches to the study of language. For example, the examination of the corpus of urban photojournalistic images in Chapter 5 has had 'imposed' upon it to some extent a polarized construal of representational practice. This might be criticized by the ethnomethodologists as being too close to everyday commonsense views of the world and that first-hand observation of photographer and subject interaction and exchange might reveal a more valid explanation than the documentary-type of 'code' approach adopted in Chapter 5. However, Bourdieusian analysis is fundamentally class analysis, and in its deployment in cultural and linguistic analysis it is about practices of classification; therefore, we have to look to the structures lying beyond the actual photograph or interactional occasion in which any one image is created in order to interpret them. This, ultimately, means understanding the press photograph as the product of broader relations of symbolic power – something that an audience focus itself would not particularly enhance.

The question of reception, audiences and practice may also be raised in the form – 'what about Wittgenstein?' The work of the 'later' Wittgenstein of the *Philosophical Investigations* would appear to be central to debates on language and practice. However, the essays contained in *Language and Symbolic Power* do not address this work because Bourdieu's thoughts on language were directed to two main challenges, the powerful (at that time) influence of structuralism, and ethnomethodology. Wittgenstein is an importance source in relation to Bourdieu's concern to substitute the idea of 'strategy' for 'rules' in studying the logic of practice. Bourdieu does articulate Wittgenstein's argument that the rules of linguistics are not the rules of language – what 'Wittgenstein would term [...] the danger of taking as a predicate something that is merely a mode of representation' (Bouveresse 1999: 76–7). However, the critical issue for Wittgenstein is that rules are intuitive and evoked in contexts, and are implicit in these to some extent, enabling us 'to go on' in linguistic (and other) practices. This is where Bourdieu departs from Wittgenstein because it is a position on language (characteristically appealing to ethnomethodologists and interactionists) that suggests we can all simply draw on 'members' resources' freely and equally, which Bourdieu's class analysis of language cannot accept.

The question of audiences is also one of the status of more empirical study of reception. Where Bourdieu's ideas have been deployed in more empirical research, such as by Henderson (Henderson et al. 2002), ideas of struggle and class competition over technological artefacts like mobiles, and by implication, language itself, have been facilitated by ideas of social (and other forms of) capital. The logic of linguistic practices in the media and new communication technologies like the mobile phone suggests that this is an important focus for more empirically focused and theoretically led observational research into social differences in the acquisition of digital media as much as the larger, theoretically led, concerns over how language, symbolic power and violence occur in the media.

However, the theoretical considerations of this book have been 'evidenced' in a number of ways: the use of news reports, photojournalism, the views of individuals involved in radio and so on. So these more empirical concerns have indicated the applicability of Bourdieu's ideas to the study of reception and audiences. For example, the concern with a non-essentialized understanding of the concept of 'voice' and the need to challenge traditional concepts of community with more hybridized ones (Chapter 6) are aspects of this. And one of the more striking developments in the case of spoken language and youth culture in recent years has been the popular takeup of Afro-Caribbean registers or accents in the stylization of talk of white working-class youth – there is no need to 'prove' this. Caribbean Carnival Radio can be seen as an early example of this trend (the original study was in 1999), one of its sources, working through a more uncommon cultural form (soca-calypso) than in (its usual association with) rap and hip hop.

The idea of this accent in its wider articulation as perhaps a generational 'voice' in white working-class youth today, shows that thinking about voice in a relational way can counter essentializing accounts like those of sociolinguistics or postmodern assumptions of 'hybridity'. Thus we saw that Hall argued that we should see voice as 'enunciation' that must be 'placed' (Hall 1991), but it might be better to see this place as fundamentally socio-structural, as an aspect of strategy and struggle, rather than essentially geographical. The burden of Chapter 6 is to show voice as a 'strategy', sometimes as 'mimicry' (on the part of the community broadcasters or in commercial stations' DJs who assume accents in a populist way), instead of something that is in a representational relationship with identity or, even, entirely to be accounted for by the idea of the habitus. So Chapter 6 does not articulate voice as an 'expression' of identity, but actually shows its meaning as arising from the dynamic and fluctuating nature of the field that gives it space for expression. As Agha notes, in this respect the idea of 'sociolect' should perhaps be used to indicate the constantly relational and rhetorical aspects to dialect, accent and voice – their 'characterological value' (Agha 2003: 232–44). Nevertheless, there are real limits to strategy and hybridity due to the embodied nature of speech and other forms of linguistic expression and this can be seen in the major problems commercial radio and the media constantly encounter when attempting to address mass audiences today. So, although there may be no need to 'prove' the trend to mimic this accent in today's youth, the 'burden of proof' of this chapter, seen in the quoted opinions of agents in the field, suggests how more empirical study into the reception side of Bourdieu's approach might be made.

The question of audiences is something that might on the surface be more easily addressed by sociolinguistic accounts like Coupland's (2001) or where detailed exchanges between DJs, for example, and audiences are shown. But the significance of relations of class and language and reception in the media arises to some extent 'externally', in seeing the dynamic 'shuffling' that arises due to the logic of tension between the various positions in the field, rather than in an 'internal' analysis of the particular forms of discourse (at the level of the sentence) or exchanges in real time. The 'plane' of explanation arising from adopting Bourdieu's approach is, as he suggested, at a theoretical remove from the technicizing-empiricist approaches within sociolinguistics and conversational analysis, but one which nevertheless is worth 'the higher price for truth'.

Thus, even where this book's analysis has appeared to 'demonstrate' linguistic violence operating 'in' texts, such as the chapters on city press journalism and photojournalism, the structures revealed are essentially relational ones. The deployment of the idea of paralogism, or the class and space codings discerned in photojournalism may seem to be forms of internal analysis, but their key status is as concepts deployed in relational analysis. So I doubt that the substantive argument of these chapters could have been improved by analysis of a greater number of images and reports, or by adopting, for example, Kress and Leeuwen's multimodal approach (Kress and Leeuwen 2001) which warns of abstracting images and reports from their overall 'page' or other so-called 'textual contexts'.

The question of reception also initiates methodological issues about the actual language of social inquiry. Thus, it might be remarked that if Bourdieu was indeed conscious of the methodological need to engage with the very language of social inquiry, such as in opinion bids, why did he not address the actual language of his surveys of museum visiting or in his anthropology of modern French culture in *Distinction*?

There is to some extent a lack of guidance by Bourdieu in methodological terms on the problem of the language of social research even though the burden of his criticisms of standard language and his sympathy with subordinated language communities suggest this concern. But the chapters on polls and text messaging deploy Bourdieu's ideas on language in these new areas of digital media and mobile telephony to show how the language of inquiry can be developed.

Finally, in relation to whether we can account for lay-reflexivity in language if we have not actually seen examples of lay discourses, Chapter 3 argues that agents achieve measures of reflexivity due to the expressive nature of 'voice' and this was demonstrated in Chapter 6 on radio. This was allied to Bakhtinian ideas of polyphony and 'polyvocality' (Guilianotti 2005) and how 'code swapping' (Coupland 2001) in spoken language impinges on the awareness of speakers, even if this awareness is, in the 'final instance', due to the social shaping of the field or any particular individual's habitus. This awareness also has an analytical purpose as well as helping us to point to elements that might be considered agency in language practices. As the discussion of the language of polling noted, an awareness of class registers in language and how people are likely to 'reinterpret' questions according to their linguistic habitus suggests a type of reflexivity.

As in relation to the issue of reception, the concern here is with demonstration and evidence. But besides the occasional exception like Hutchby who articulates ideas like 'affordances' (Hutchby 2006), more empirically based approaches like ethnomethodology still miss how the media provides discursive grounds for reflexivity or intentionality of a form that is uniquely indexical to it. This is because they see indexicality in Wittgensteinian terms as ultimately dependent on more general, universal, constants in communication (as discussed in Chapter 3). But, as mentioned in relation to Couldry's work (Couldry 2003), the media provides perhaps a key ground in modern societies in which lay and elite discourses interact, and in that sense 'the action' will be indexical to that ground. This understanding underlies the studies of radio and text messaging of this book, a concern to demonstrate how – within the space of modern media and communication technologies – traditional understandings of class and language (such as the evaluative attitudes to regional accents) are actually articulated in discursive struggles there.

The nature of symbolic violence in the language of the media discussed in Chapters 4 and 5 and elsewhere in this book is also suggestive of another 'practical' aspect of reflexivity – journalists' appreciation of their own ethical codes. The critical burden of these chapters is that it is in the language of the press and other forms of journalistic media where technical and instrumentalist forms of discourse are often initially subjected to 'ethical-moral' reflection and debate (in Habermasian parlance) – for example, the rights and wrongs of any particular urban development. For Bourdieu, particularly in the essays on journalism contained in his *Political Interventions*, the aim of critique was to promote this type of 'sociological break' in their everyday practices and promote reflexivity – a very 'empirical' concern.

Admittedly, the concern of this book's third theme with lay-reflexivity might suggest that more direct quoting from research on audiences and consumers was needed to support this idea. But ideas of lay-reflexivity have been articulated here in theoretical terms in order to ameliorate the overly objectivist interpretations of Bourdieu's sociology, and to make links with the 'subjectivism' in approaches like ethnomethodology. It is an aim of this book to 'bring out' of Bourdieu the influence that Husserl's phenomenology has had on his work. His work has as a whole sociologized – objectified – seemingly more 'subjective' phenomenological tenets such as the 'transcendental reduction' and made them operationalizable ideas like the 'second' or 'epistemic break'. But Chapter 7 on opinion polling does show how the ideas can be made to work in the analysis of media and language. Bourdieu's criticisms of polling agencies' understanding of opinion are based on pervasively Husserlian ideas about the relationship between scientific and ordinary language (seen in Husserl's *Crisis of the Human Sciences and Transcendental Philosophy*). But if his ideas turn on some of the axes provided by Husserl he nevertheless shows how to operationalize them sociologically, methodologically and politically.

Often Bourdieu was 'in denial' of his sympathy for lay actors: for example, in his discussion with Terry Eagleton he comes across as somewhat dismissive of the possibility that lay or working-class people more generally could attain levels of reflexivity (Bourdieu and Eagleton 1999). It may be that we can see language as the fundamental symbolic material in which doxa or reflexivity, symbolic domination or symbolic reflection, might be revealed – by quoting lay actors' words. But Bourdieu's concern with Don't Knows in polls is an expression of his more complex understanding of lay-reflexivity as something that is often 'beyond words' themselves. As we have noted at many points in this book, Bourdieu often locates agency in the body rather than in the intellect, in the habitus. This aspect, essentially drawn from Merleau-Ponty's reading of Husserl, means that what we usually expect in terms of agency, intellectual enlightenment or its exposition in speech, is often missing in Bourdieu's accounts and this has from the inception of his work brought criticisms of sociological determinism (Jenkins 2002).

But, finally, this book has sought to show how Bourdieu alerts us to take as sociologically significant the kind of 'break-outs' or 'failures to agree' with or recognize the legitimacy of dominant ways of looking at the world. This is why so often language bucks against its standardized forms, in texts or in polls, and presents its would-be legislators with the problem of linguistic-types of 'going absent without leave' (Böll 1995) and intuitive forms of saying no to those official sources that Tony Harrison has called the 'Receivers' of the language. More often than not our intuitive denials of 'the rules' of language are embodied in our dispositions which act like an ur-spring for more of our linguistic practices than quoted words can ever represent.

References

Adkins, L. and Skeggs, B. (eds) 2004. *Feminism After Bourdieu*, Oxford: Blackwell.

Agha, A. 2003. 'The Social Life of Cultural Value', *Language and Communication* 23(3–4): 231–73.

Albert-Honore, S. 1992. 'Empowered Voices: Freedom of Expression and Afro-American Radio', doctoral thesis, University of Michigan.

Alexander, J.C. 2008. *The Civil Sphere*, New York and Oxford: Oxford University Press.

Althaus, S.L. 2003. *Collective Preferences in Democratic Politics: Opinion Surveys and the Will of the People*, Cambridge: Cambridge University Press.

Atkinson, P. 1999. 'Voiced and Unvoiced', *British Journal of Sociology* 33(1): 191–8.

Auer, P. and Hinskins, F. 2005. 'The Role of Interpersonal Communication in a Theory of Language Change', in P. Auer and F. Hinskins (eds), *Dialect Change*, Cambridge: Cambridge University Press.

Austin, J.L. 1975. *How to do Things with Words*, Cambridge, MA: Harvard University Press.

Bakhtin, M.M. and Holquist, M.E. 1981. *The Dialogic Imagination: Four Essays*, Austin: University of Texas Press.

Baron, N.S. 2000. *Alphabet to Email: How Written English Evolved and Where It's Heading*, London: Routledge.

——2008. *Always On: Language in an Online and Mobile World*, Oxford: Oxford University Press.

Barthes, R. 1977. *Image, Music Text*, London: Flamingo, 1984.

——1981. *Camera Lucida: Reflections on Photography*, London: Flamingo, 1984.

Beal, J.C. 2006. *Language and Region*, London: Routledge.

Bender, J.F. 1951. *NBC Handbook of Pronunciation*, 2nd edition, New York: Crowell.

Benson, R.D. 2004. 'Bringing the Sociology of the Media Back In', *Political Communication* 21: 275–92.

——2006. 'News Media as a "Journalistic Field": What Bourdieu Adds to New Institutionalism and Vice Versa', *Political Communication* 23: 187–202.

Benson, R.D. and Neveu, E. 2005. *Bourdieu and the Journalistic Field*, Cambridge: Polity Press.

Berinsky, A.J. 2004. *Silent Voices: Public Opinion and Political Participation in America*, Princeton, NJ and Oxford: Princeton University Press.

Bhabha, H.K. 1994. *The Location of Culture*, London and New York: Routledge, 2004.

Blanchot, M. 1993. *The Infinite Conversation*, Minneapolis: University of Minnesota Press.

Boden, D. and Zimmerman, D.H. 1991. *Talk and Social Structure: Studies in Ethnomethodology and Conversation Analysis*, Cambridge: Polity Press.
Böll, H. 1995. *Absent Without Leave*, Evanston, IL: Northwestern University Press.
Bourdieu, P. 1977. *Outline of a Theory of Practice*, Cambridge: Cambridge University Press.
——1984. *Distinction: a Social Critique of the Judgement of Taste*, London: Routledge & Kegan Paul.
——1990a. *Homo Academicus*, Cambridge: Polity Press.
——1990b. *In Other Words: Essays Towards a Reflexive Sociology*, Cambridge: Polity Press.
——1990c. *Photography: a Middle-brow Art*, Cambridge: Polity Press.
——1993a. *The Field of Cultural Production: Essays on Art and Literature*, Cambridge: Polity Press.
——1993b. *Sociology in Question*, London: Sage.
——1998. *On Television and Journalism*, London: Pluto.
—— 1999. *The Weight of the World: Social Suffering in Contemporary Society*, Cambridge: Polity Press.
——2000. *Pascalian Meditations*, Cambridge: Polity Press.
——2004. *Science of Science and Reflexivity*, Cambridge: Polity Press.
——2005. 'The Political Field, the Social Science Field, and the Journalistic Field', in R.D. Benson (ed.), *Bourdieu and the Journalistic Field*, Cambridge: Polity Press.
Bourdieu, P. and Eagleton, T. 1999. 'Doxa and Common Life: an Interview', in S. Žižek (ed.), *Mapping Ideology*, London: Verso.
Bourdieu, P. and Passeron, J.-C. 1963. 'Sociologues des Mythologies et Mythologies de Sociologues', *Les Temps Modernes* 211: 998–1021.
Bourdieu, P., Passeron, J.-C. and Saint Martin, M.D. 1994. *Academic Discourse: Linguistic Misunderstanding and Professorial Power*, Cambridge: Polity Press.
Bourdieu, P., Poupeau, F. and Discepolo, T. 2008. *Political Interventions: Social Science and Political Action*, London: Verso.
Bourdieu, P. and Thompson, J.B. 1991. *Language and Symbolic Power*, Cambridge: Polity Press.
Bourdieu, P. and Wacquant, L.C.J.D. 1992. *Invitation to Reflexive Sociology*, Cambridge: Polity Press.
——2001. 'Neo-Liberal Newspeak: Notes on a New Planetary Vulgate', *Radical Philosophy* 108.
Bouveresse, J. 1999. 'Rules, Dispositions and the Habitus', in R. Shusterman (ed.), *Bourdieu: a Critical Reader*, Oxford: Blackwell.
Bowler, S. and Donovan, T. 1998. *Demanding Choices: Opinion, Voting, and Direct Democracy*, Ann Arbor: University of Michigan Press.
Burchfield, R.W., Donoghue, D. and Timothy, A. 1979. *The Quality of Spoken English on BBC Radio: a Report for the BBC*, London: British Broadcasting Corporation.
Burgin, V. 1982. *Thinking Photography*, London: Macmillan.

——1997. 'Common Sense and Photography', in J. Evans (ed.), *The Camerawork Essays: Context and Meaning in Photography*, London: Rivers Oram.

Butler, J. 1997. *Excitable Speech: a Politics of the Performative*, New York and London: Routledge.

Calhoun, C.J., Lipuma, E. and Postone, M. 1993. *Bourdieu: Critical Perspectives*, Cambridge: Polity Press.

Callewaert, S. 2006. 'Bourdieu, Critic of Foucault', *Theory, Culture, Society* 23(6): 73–98.

Castells, M. and Hall, P.G. 1994. *Technopoles of the World: the Making of Twenty-First-Century Industrial Complexes*, London: Routledge.

Castells, M. and Lebas, E. 1978. *City, Class and Power*, London: Macmillan.

Champagne, P. 1990. *Faire l'opinion: le Nouveau Jeu Politique*, Paris: Editions Minuit.

——1999. 'The View from the Media', in P. Bourdieu (ed.), *The Weight of the World*, Cambridge: Polity Press.

——2005. 'Making the People Speak', in L. Wacquant (ed.), *Bourdieu and Democratic Politics*, Oxford: Blackwell.

Champagne, P. and Marchetti, D. 2005. 'The Contaminated Blood Scandal', in R. Benson and E. Neveu (eds), *Bourdieu and the Media*, Cambridge: Polity Press.

Charlesworth, S.J. 2000. *A Phenomenology of Working-Class Experience*, Cambridge: Cambridge University Press.

Chouliaraki, L. and Fairclough, N. 1999a. *Discourse in Late Modernity: Rethinking Critical Discourse Analysis*, Edinburgh: Edinburgh University Press.

——1999b. 'Language and Power in Bourdieu: a Response to Hasan's "The Disempowerment Game"', *Linguistics and Education* 10(4): 399–409.

Coates, J. and Cameron, D. 1989. *Women in Their Speech Communities: New Perspectives on Language and Sex*, London: Longman.

Couldry, N. 2000. *The Place of Media Power: Pilgrims and Witnesses of the Media Age*, London: Routledge.

——2003a. 'Media Meta-Capital: Extending the Range of Bourdieu's Field Theory', *Theory and Society* 32(5–6): 653–77.

——2003b. *Media Rituals*, London: Routledge.

——2003c. *Media Rituals: a Critical Approach*, London: Routledge.

——2005. 'The Individual Point of View: Learning from Bourdieu's *The Weight of the World*', *Critical Methodologies* 5(3): 354–72.

Couldry, N. and Curran, J. 2003 *Contesting Media Power: Alternative Media in a Networked World*, Lanham, MD and Oxford: Rowman & Littlefield.

Coupland, N. 2001. 'Dialect Stylization in Radio Talk', *Language in Society* 30: 345–75.

——2008. 'The Delicate Constitution of Identity in Face-to-Face Accommodation: a Response to Trudgill', *Language in Society* 37(2): 267–70.

Crossley, N. 2004. 'On Systematically Distorted Communication: Bourdieu and the Socio-Analysis of Publics', in N. Crossley (ed.), *After Habermas*, Oxford: Blackwell.

Crowley, T. 2003. *Standard English and the Politics of Language*, 2nd edition, Basingstoke: Palgrave Macmillan.

Crystal, D. 2001. *Language and the Internet*, Cambridge: Cambridge University Press.

——2008a. '2b Or Not 2b', *The Guardian*, 5 July.

——2008b. *Txtng: The Gr8 Db8*, Oxford: Oxford University Press.

Davidson, A. 2004. 'Reinhabiting Technology', *Technology in Society* 26: 85–97.

Davis, M. 2006. *City of Quartz: Excavating the Future in Los Angeles*, new edition, London and New York: Verso.

Denselow, R. 1989. *When the Music's Over: the Story of Political Pop*, London: Faber.

Derrida, J., Leavey, J.P., Allison, D.B. and Husserl, E.O.O.G. 1978. *Edmund Husserl's 'Origin of Geometry': an Introduction*, New York: N. Hays and [Hassocks]: Harvester Press.

Douglas, J.D. 1971. *Understanding Everyday Life*, London: Routledge & Kegan Paul.

Drijvers, J. 1992. 'Community Broadcasting: a Manifesto for the Media Policy of Small European Countries', *Media, Culture, Society* 14: 193–201.

Dudley, S. 1996. '"Judging by the Beat": Calypso Versus Soca', *Journal of Ethnomusicology* (Spring/Summer): 269–98.

Dunaway, D. 1998. 'Community Radio or the Legitimacy of the 20th Century: Commercialism Versus Community Power', *Javnost–The Public* 5(2): 87–103.

Fairclough, N. 2001. *Language and Power*, 2nd edition, Harlow: Longman.

——2003. *Analysing Discourse: Textual Analysis for Social Research*, London: Routledge.

Forester, J. 1993. *Critical Theory, Public Policy, and Planning Practice: Toward a Critical Pragmatism*, Albany: State University of New York Press.

Fortunati, L. 2002. 'The Mobile Phone: Towards New Categories and Social Relations', *Information, Communication and Society* 5(4): 513–28.

Foucault, M., Fitzpatrick, J. P. S. K. C. M. G. and Smith, A. M. S. P. 1972. *The Archaeology of Knowledge*, trans. A. M. Sheridan Smith, London: Tavistock Publications.

Fowler, H.W. *Fowler's Modern English Usage: With an Introduction by Simon Winchester*, Oxford: Oxford University Press, 1926 (2002 printing).

Franklin, B. and Murphy, D. 1991. *What News? The Market, Politics and the Local Press*, London: Routledge.

Gardiner, M.E. 2004. 'Wild Publics and Grotesque Symposiums', in N. Crossley and J.M. Roberts (eds), *After Habermas*, Oxford: Blackwell.

Gibson, E.J. and Pick, A.D. 2000. *An Ecological Approach to Perceptual Learning and Development*, New York: Oxford University Press.

Giles, H., Coupland, J. and Coupland, N. 1991. *Contexts of Accommodation: Developments in Applied Sociolinguistics*, Cambridge: Cambridge University Press.

Gilroy, P. 2000 *Between Camps: Race, Identity and Nationalism at the End of the Colour Line*, London: Allen Lane.

Ginsberg, B. 1989. 'How Polling Transforms Public Opinion', in M. Margolis (ed.), *Manipulating Public Opinion*, Pacific Grove: Brooks/Cole.

Goffman, E. 1979. *Gender Advertisements*, London: Macmillan.
——1981. *Forms of Talk*, Oxford: Blackwell.
Goggin, G. 2004. '"Mobile Text"', *M/C*, Vol. 2008.
Gouldner, A.W. 1979. *The Future of Intellectuals and the Rise of the New Class*, London: Macmillan.
Gowers, E.S. 1948. *Plain Words: a Guide to the Use of English*, [S. L.]: HMSO.
Graham, S. 1997. 'Urban Planning and the Information City', *Town and Country Planning*.
Gray, P. and Lewis, P.M. 1992. 'Community Broadcasting Revisited', in N.W. Jankowski (ed.), *The People's Voice*, London: John Libbey.
Green, N. 2003. 'Outwardly Mobile: Young People and Mobile Technologies', in J.E. Katz (ed.), *Machines That Become Us*, New Brunswick, NJ: Transaction Books.
Guilianotti, R. 2005. 'Towards a Critical Anthropology of Voice: the Politics and Poets of Popular Culture, Scotland and Football', *Critique of Anthropology* 25(4): 339–59.
Habermas, J. 1991. *The Theory of Communicative Action*: Cambridge: Polity Press.
Habermas, J., Crossley, N. and Roberts, J.M. 2004. *After Habermas: New Perspectives on the Public Sphere*, Oxford, UK and Malden, MA: Blackwell Publishing/Sociological Review.
Hall, S. 1972. 'External Influences on Broadcasting', in F. S. Baddley (ed.), *4th Symposium on Broadcasting Policies*, Manchester: University of Manchester.
——1991. 'The Local and the Global: Globalization and Ethnicity', in A. King (ed.), *Culture Globalization and the World System*, London: Routledge.
Halliday, M.A.K. 1985. *Language as Social Semiotic*, London: Arnold.
Hanks, W.F. 2005. 'Pierre Bourdieu and the Practices of Language', *Annual Review of Anthropology* 34: 67–83.
Harrasser, K. 2002. 'Transforming Discourse into Practice: Computerhystories and Digital Cultures Around 1984', *Cultural Studies* 1: 820–31.
Harris, R. 1986. *The Origin of Writing*, London: Duckworth.
Harvey, D. 1996. 'On Planning and the Ideology of Planning', in S. S. Fainstein and P. Healey (eds), *Readings in Planning Theory*, Oxford: Blackwell.
Hasan, R. 1999a. 'Bourdieu on Language and Linguistics: a Response to my Commentators', *Linguistics and Education* 10(4): 441–58.
——1999b. 'The Disempowerment Game', *Linguistics and Education* 10(1): 25–87.
Healey, P. 1995. *Managing Cities: the New Urban Context*, Chichester: John Wiley.
Heidegger, M. 1993. *Basic Writings from 'Being and Time' (1927) to 'The Task of Thinking' (1964)*, rev. and expanded edition, London: Routledge.
Henderson, S., Taylor, R. and Thomson, R. 2002. 'In Touch: Young People, Communication and Technologies', *Information, Communication and Society* 5(4): 494–512.
Herbst, S. 1993. *Numbered Voices: How Opinion Polling Has Shaped American Politics*, Chicago and London: University of Chicago Press.

——2002. 'Surveys in the Public Sphere: Applying Bourdieu's Critique of Opinion Polls', *International Journal of Public Opinion Research* 4: 220–9.

Heritage, J. 1984. *Garfinkel and Ethnomethodology*, Cambridge: Polity Press.

Hill, D.R. 1993. *Calypso Calaloo: Early Carnival Music in Trinidad*, Gainesville, FL: University Press of Florida.

Hirsch, M. 1997. *Family Frames: Photography, Narrative, and Postmemory*, Cambridge, MA and London: Harvard University Press.

Hodge, R. and Kress, G.R. 1988. *Social Semiotics*, Cambridge: Polity Press.

Hollander, E. and Stoppers, J. 1992. 'Community Media and Community Communication', in N.W. Jankowski (ed.), *The People's Voice*, London: John Libbey.

Honey, J. 1997. *Language is Power: the Story of Standard English and its Enemies*, London: Faber.

Hudson, R.A. 1980. *Sociolinguistics*, Cambridge: Cambridge University Press.

Humphreys, J. 2005. *Lost for Words: the Mangling and Manipulating of English*, London: Hodder & Stoughton.

Husserl, E., Ameriks, K., Churchill, J.S., Eley, L., Husserl, E.S.W. and Landgrebe, L. 1973. *Experience and Judgement: Investigations in a Genealogy of Logic*, revised and ed. Ludwig Landgrebe, trans. James S. Churchill and Karl Ameriks, intro. James S. Churchill, afterword Lothar Eley, London: Routledge & Kegan Paul.

Hutchby, I. 1996. *Confrontation Talk: Arguments, Asymmetries, and Power on Talk Radio*, Mahwah, NJ [Great Britain]: L. Erlbaum Associates.

——2001. *Conversation and Technology*, Cambridge: Polity Press.

——2006. *Media Talk: Conversation Analysis and the Study of Broadcasting*, Maidenhead: Open University Press.

Irvine, J.T. 1989. 'When Talk Isn't Cheap: Language and Political Economy', *American Ethnologist* 16: 248–67.

Jalbert, P.L. 1999. *Media Studies: Ethnomethodological Approaches*, Lanham, MD and Oxford: University Press of America.

Jenkins, R. 2002. *Pierre Bourdieu*, London: Routledge.

Jones, G.M. and Schieffelin, B.B. 2009. 'Talking Text and Talking Back: "My BFF Jill" from Boob Tube to Youtube', *Journal of Computer-Mediated Communication* 14: 1050–79.

Kasesniemi, E. and Rautiainen, P. 2002. 'Mobile Culture of Children and Teenagers in Finland', in J.E. Katz and M. Aakhus (eds), *Perpetual Contact*, Cambridge: Cambridge University Press.

Katznelson, I., Milner, H.V. and Finifter, A.W.P.S. 2002. *Political Science: the State of the Discipline*, ed. Ira Katznelson and Helen V. Milner, New York and London: W.W. Norton.

Keller, P. 1999. *Husserl and Heidegger on Human Experience*, Cambridge: Cambridge University Press.

Kress, G.R. 1997. *Before Writing: Rethinking the Paths to Literacy*, London: Routledge.

Kress, G.R. and Leeuwen, T.V. 2001. *Multimodal Discourse: the Modes and Media of Contemporary Communication*, London: Arnold.

Lane, J. F. 2000. *Pierre Bourdieu: a Critical Introduction*, London: Pluto.
Latour, B. 1993. *We Have Never Been Modern*, New York and London: Harvester Wheatsheaf.
Ledeneva, A. 1995. 'Language as an Instrument of Power in the Works of Pierre Bourdieu', *University of Manchester Occasional Papers* (41), Manchester: University of Manchester.
Lefebvre, H. 1991. *The Production of Space*, Oxford: Blackwell.
Lefebvre, H., Kofman, E. and Lebas, E. 1996. *Writings on Cities*, Oxford: Blackwell.
Leonard, T. 1995. *Reports from the Present*, London: Cape.
Lewis, P. M. and Booth, J. 1989. *The Invisible Medium: Public, Commercial and Community Radio*, Basingstoke: Macmillan.
Ling, R. 2004. *The Mobile Connection*, San Francisco: Morgan Kauffman.
Ling, R. and Baron, N. S. 2007. 'Text Messaging and IM: Linguistic Comparison of American College Data', *Journal of Language and Social Psychology* 26(3): 291–8.
Ling, R. and Yttri, B. 2002. 'Hyper-Coordination Via Mobile Phones in Norway', in J. E. Katz and M. Aakhus (eds), *Perpetual Contact*, Cambridge: Cambridge University Press.
Lipari, L. 2000. 'Towards a Discourse Approach to Polling', *Discourse Studies* 2(2): 187–215.
Lipi-Green, R. 1998. *English with an Accent*, London: Routledge.
Little, A. C., Burris, R., Jones, B. and Roberts, S. 2007. 'Facial Appearance Affects Voting Decisions', *Evolution and Human Behaviour* 28: 18–27.
Logan, J. R. and Molotch, H. L. 1987. *Urban Fortunes: the Political Economy of Place*, Berkeley and London: University of California Press.
Lovell, T. 2004. 'Bourdieu, Class and Gender: the Return of the Living Dead?' in L. Adkins and B. Skeggs (eds), *Feminism After Bourdieu*, Oxford: Blackwell.
Mann, T. E. and Orren, G. R. 1992. *Media Polls in American Politics*, Washington, DC: Brookings Institution.
Margolis, M. and Mauser, G. A. (eds) 1989. *Manipulating Public Opinion: Essays on Public Opinion as a Dependent Variable*, Pacific Grove, CA: Brooks/Cole Publishing Co.
Marlière, P. 1998. 'The Rules of the Journalistic Field: Pierre Bourdieu's Contribution to the Sociology of Media', *European Journal of Communication* 13(2): 219–34.
——2000. 'The Impact of Market Journalism: Pierre Bourdieu on the Media', in B. Fowler (ed.), *Reading Bourdieu on Society and Culture*, Oxford: Blackwell.
Matheson, D. 2003. 'Scowling at their Notebooks: How British Journalists Understand their Writing', *Journalism* 4(2): 165–83.
McDowell, L. 2000. 'Learning to Serve? Employment Aspirations and Attitudes of Young Working Class Men in an Era of Labour Market Restructuring', *Gender, Place and Culture* 7: 389–416.
McLuhan, M. 1967. *The Gutenberg Galaxy*, London: Routledge & Kegan Paul.
——2001. *Understanding Media: the Extensions of Man*, London: Routledge.

Merrifield, A. and Swyngedouw, E. 1997. *The Urbanization of Injustice*, Washington Square: New York University Press.

Meyer, P. 1979. *Precision Journalism: a Reporter's Introduction to Social Science Methods*, 2nd edition, Bloomington and London: Indiana University Press.

Meyer, T. and Hinchman, L. 2002. *Media Democracy: How the Media Colonize Politics*, Oxford: Polity Press.

Montgomery, M. 1986. 'DJ Talk', *Media, Culture, Society* 8(4): 421–40.

Moss, P. and Higgins, C. 1984. 'Radio Voices', *Media, Culture, Society* 6: 353–75.

Myers, G. 2005. 'Applied Linguists and Institutions of Opinion', *Applied Linguistics* 26(4): 527–44.

Myles, J. 2004. 'From Doxa to Experience: Issues in Bourdieu's Adoption of Husserlian Phenomenology', *Theory, Culture and Society* 21(2): 91–107.

——2007. 'Making Don't Knows Make Sense: Bourdieu, Phenomenology and Opinion Polls', *Sociological Review* 56(1): 102–16.

Negt, O. and Kluge, A. 1993. *Public Sphere and Experience: Toward an Analysis of the Bourgeois and Proletarian Public Sphere*, Minneapolis: University of Minnesota Press.

Newbury, D. 1997. 'Talking About Practice: Photography Students, Photographic Culture and Professional Identities', *British Journal of Sociology of Education* 18(3): 421–34.

Ong, W.J. 1982. *Orality and Literacy: the Technologizing of the Word*, London: Methuen.

Page, B. and Tannenbaum, J. 1996. 'Populist Deliberation and Radio Talk', *Journal of Communication* 46(2): 33–54.

Peterson, J.H. 2003. 'Lipmann Revisited: a Comment 80 Years Subsequent to "Public Opinion"', *Journalism* 4(2): 249–59.

Plant, S. 2001. 'On the Mobile: the Effects of Mobile Telephones on Social and Individual Life', Vol. 2008: Motorola.

Poupeau, F. 2000. 'Reasons for Domination: Bourdieu versus Habermas', in B. Fowler (ed.), *Reading Bourdieu on Society and Culture*, Oxford: Blackwell.

Rheingold, H. 2000. *The Virtual Community: Homesteading on the Electronic Frontier*, rev. edition, Cambridge, MA and London: MIT Press.

—— 2002 *Smart Mobs: the Next Social Revolution*, Cambridge, MA: Perseus.

Robbins, D. 2006. *Bourdieu, Education and Society*, Oxford: Bardwell Press.

Robinson, M. 2001. *Mobocracy: How the Media's Obsession with Polling Twists the News, Alters Elections, and Undermines Democracy*, Roseville, CA: Prima.

Russell, A. 2007. 'Digital Communication Networks and the Journalistic Field: the 2005 French Riots', *Critical Studies in Media Communication* 24(4): 285–302.

Saussure, F.D., Bally, C., Sechehaye, A., Riedlinger, A. and Harris, R. 1983. *Course in General Linguistics*, London: Duckworth.

Scannell, P. 1989. 'Public Service Broadcasting and Modern Public Life', *Media, Culture, Society* 11: 135–56.

——1991. *Broadcast Talk*, London: Sage Publications.

Schegloff, E.A. 1997. 'Whose Text? Whose Context?' *Discourse and Society* 8(2): 165–87.

Schultz, I. 2007. 'The Journalistic Gut Feeling', *Journalism Practice* 1(2): 190–207.

Schuman, H. and Presser, S. 1996. *Questions and Answers in Attitude Surveys: Experiments on Question Form, Wording, and Context*, Thousand Oaks, CA and London: Sage.

Scollon, R. 2001. *Mediated Discourse*, London: Routledge.

Sekula, A. 1981. 'On the Invention of Photographic Meaning', in V. Goldberg (ed.), *Photography in Print: Writings from 1816 to the Present*, New York: Simon & Schuster.

Smith, L. 1998. *The Politics of Focus: Women, Children, and Nineteenth-Century Photography*, Manchester: Manchester University Press.

Solomon-Godeau, A. 1991. *Photography at the Dock: Essays on Photographic History, Institutions, and Practices*, Minneapolis: University of Minnesota Press.

Spagnolli, A. and Gamberini, L. 2007. 'Interacting via SMS: Practices of Social Closeness and Reciprocation', *British Journal of Social Psychology* 46(2): 343–64.

Spence, J. 1995. *Cultural Sniping: the Art of Transgression*, London: Routledge.

Sterne, J. 2003. 'Bourdieu, Technique and Technology', *Cultural Studies* 17(3/4): 367–89.

Strauss, C. 2004. 'Cultural Standing in Expression of Opinion', *Language in Society* 33: 161–94.

Sutcliffe, D.M.E. 1984. 'British Black English and West Indian Creoles', in P. Trudgill (ed.), *Language in the British Isles*, Cambridge: Cambridge University Press.

TalkTalk. 2008. 'Digital Anthropology Report'.

Text.It. 2009. 'Latest Text Figures', Vol. 2009.

Thurlow, C. 2002/3. 'Generation Txt? The Sociolinguistics of Young People's Text-Messaging', *Discourse Analysis Online*, Vol. 2008.

Troop, C.J. and Murphy, K.M. 2002. 'Bourdieu and Phenomenology: a Critical Assessment', *Anthropological Theory* 2: 185–207.

Trudgill, P. 1990. *Dialects of England*, Oxford: Blackwell.

Truss, L. and Timmons, B. 2006. *Eats, Shoots & Leaves: Why, Commas Really DO Make A Difference!* London: Profile.

Urry, J. 2007. *Mobilities*, Cambridge: Polity Press.

Wacquant, L.J.D. and Bourdieu, P. 2005. *Pierre Bourdieu and Democratic Politics: the Mystery of Ministry*, Cambridge: Polity Press.

Wahl-Jorgensen, K. 2007. *Journalists and the Public*, New Jersey: Hampton Press.

Walker, J.A. and Chaplin, S. 1997. *Visual Culture: an Introduction*, Manchester: Manchester University Press.

Wall, T. 1998. 'Radio and Black Music in America and Britain', *Association of Media, Culture and Communication*, Sheffield Hallam University.

Weider, D.L. 1974. *Language and Social Reality*, The Hague: Mouton.

Weigel, S. 1996 *Body- and Image-Space: Re-Reading Walter Benjamin*, London: Routledge.

Willis, P. 1972. *Learning to Labour*, Aldershot: Gower.
Work Foundation. 2003. 'Mobile UK: Mobile Phones and Everyday Life', Vol. 2008.
Zelizer, B. 1993. 'Pioneers and Plain Folks: Cultural Constructions of "Place" in Radio News', *Semiotica* 3–4: 269–85.

Index

Page numbers in **bold** indicate figures, tables and boxes.

journalism, journalists and
    Bourdieu – *continued*
    ideal role in planning, 75–6
    linguistic discourse, 26
    news generating, 111
    paralogism, 3–4, 55–77
    political role, 56, 78
    reflexivity, 59–60, 73, 151
    regional print media, 56
    relative rationality, 74–6
    standards or usage, 146
    see also news reports, textual
        analysis; 'paralogism'; planning
        and urban regeneration;
        reporting urban regeneration

Kantianism and Bourdieu, 74, 75,
    76, 120, 123
Kasesniemi, E., 142
Klinenberg, E., 28
Kluge, A, 76
Krassner, Paul, 17
Kress, G. R., 149

language
    and Bourdieu, 2, 9
    as embodied practice, 124
    field, 124
    non-standard forms, 152
    oral nature of, 10
    postmodernist criticism, 37–40
    practice, parole and symbolic
        power, 33
    social context, 74–5
    and social difference, 14
    social distinction, 10
    and social forces, 34
    and social practice, 36
    and social structure, 35, 40–1
    sociolinguistic approach, 45, 51,
        149, 150
    standardization of, 17–20
    symbolic power and media, 9, 30–1
    symbolic violence and social
        justice, 74–5
    and textual practice, 34–6

    see also 'field', linguistic; spoken
        language, social variations;
        Standard English
language, media and Bourdieu,
    studies of, 23–31
    Benson, 28
    Benson and Neveu, 23–5, 26
    Champagne, 26–7
    Couldry, 9, 30–1
    Marlière, 27
    Matheson, 29–30
    Schultz, 29
language technologies, and society,
    124
Latour, B., 132
lay actors and voice, 76, 148, 150
    break out of constraints, 145
    challenge to symbolic violence, 3
    exclusion of, 61–2, 144
    focus on, 3
    inclusion in the media, 73–4
    and the media, 31
    reflexivity, 2, 46, 48, 49, 51, 55,
        61–2, 75–6, 110, 150, 151–2
    symbolic power, 49
Lebas, E., 70, 92
Leeuwen, T. V., 149
Lefebvre, H., 76, 84, 91
Lewis, P. M., 101
Lidell, Alver, 19
Ling, R., 141, 142
linguistic 'market', 15, 17–19, 21,
    144, 145–6
Lipari, L., 117–18
Lippman, Walter, 5
Logan, J. R., 57
Lovell, T., 39–40

Manchester, Caribbean Carnival
    Radio, 96–100
Mandelson, Peter, 119
'market' concept, 28
    see also linguistic 'market'
Marlière, P., 27
Matheson, D., 29–30
McCullin, Don, 79